West's

Essentials of

Microsoft® Visual Basic®

Jonathan C. Barron
Associate Professor of Mathematics
Eastern College
St. Davids, Pennsylvania

WEST PUBLISHING COMPANY
Minneapolis/St. Paul • New York
Los Angeles • San Francisco

WEST'S COMMITMENT TO THE ENVIRONMENT

In 1906, West Publishing Company began recycling materials left over from the production of books. This began a tradition of efficient and responsible use of resources. Today, up to 95 percent of our legal books and 70 percent of our college and school texts are printed on recycled, acid-free stock. West also recycles nearly 22 million pounds of scrap paper annually—the equivalent of 181,717 trees. Since the 1960s, West has devised ways to capture and recycle waste inks, solvents, oils, and vapors created in the printing process. We also recycle plastics of all kinds, wood, glass, corrugated cardboard, and batteries, and have eliminated the use of Styrofoam book packaging. We at West are proud of the longevity and the scope of our commitment to the environment.

Production, Prepress, Printing and Binding by West Publishing Company
Project Management by Labrecque Publishing Services

 Text Is Printed on 10% Post Consumer Recycled Paper

Microsoft® and Visual Basic® are registered trademarks of Microsoft Corporation.

Library of Congress Cataloging-in-Publication Data

Barron, Jonathan C.
    West's essentials of Microsoft Visual Basic / Jonathan C. Barron.
        p.   cm. – (The Microcomputing series)
    Includes index.
    ISBN 0-314-05531-2
        1. BASIC (Computer program language)   2. Microsoft Visual BASIC.
I. Title.   II. Series
QA76.73.B3B364 1995   94-49431
005.26'2–dc20   CIP

British Library Cataloguing-in-Publication Data. A catalogue record for this book is available from the British Library.

Contents

Preface

West's Essentials of Visual Basic is an introduction to the fundamentals of programming using the Visual Basic Programming System for Windows. Every element of traditional Basic programming, such as loops and decision structures, is introduced and amply illustrated. The methods of structured programming and modularization are combined by subdividing programs into a series of smaller, more manageable, tasks, and then programming each task separately as a procedure, using only the logic constructs of structured programming (sequence, loop, and decision). Consequently, no previous programming experience is required.

However, the book goes much further by introducing you to event-driven programming. This is where the real power of Visual Basic comes to the fore. In traditional programming, a program is executed starting with the first line of code, and then proceeds through the rest of the program according to dictates of the program—that is, *the program is in control*. The only thing a user might do is enter some data during the process. Otherwise, the run continues on its own. On the other hand, a Visual Basic program is event-driven—that is, *the user is in control*. Your code is only executed as a result of an event initiated by the user or, in some cases, by the system itself. You draw the user interface (what the user sees on the screen at run time) using objects called controls, such as command buttons. These controls allow the user (not the program) to determine which code is executed next. We introduce many, but by no means all, of the important features of Visual Basic.

The book uses a spiral approach by beginning with simple programs and gradually building to more complex ones. In my view, the best way to get you excited about programming is to give you "hands on" experience as quickly as possible, using interesting, meaningful examples. For this reason, we begin each project (a term used by Microsoft to refer to the entire process of creating a Visual Basic program) with a particular application in mind—that is, something we want to know and we could use a computer to find. For example, we might try something like converting Celsius temperatures to Fahrenheit. Next, we discuss the necessary Visual Basic keywords and programming techniques needed to write the required Basic code. To finish, we decide what objects, and their properties, are required for our user interface. Thus, you are introduced to Visual Basic through a series of examples that are completely designed and explained before being coded. You will learn about the many exciting features of Visual Basic by actually using them to create various applications.

Each unit contains several Guided Activities that you should complete while sitting at the computer. These activities are designed to enhance your understanding of the Visual Basic keywords and programming techniques introduced in the unit, as well as to help you become familar with the Visual Basic environment.

Unit 1 begins by introducing a sufficient number of Visual Basic statements to have you writing your own projects by the end of the unit. Unit 2 presents more about interfaces and explores the Print method and formatting output. Unit 3 details the concept of a loop, with all types of loop structures discussed and illustrated. Unit 4 offers more information on how data is supplied to a program by means of a sequential file. Unit 5 rounds out the introduction to the fundamentals of Visual Basic programming by covering decision structures such as the block If/Then/Else statement. Unit 6 introduces data structures and subscripted variables.

The text contains a wide variety of Exercises from which to choose and, we hope, you will find something relevant to your particular interests.

West's Essentials of Visual Basic is a part of THE MICROCOMPUTING SERIES published by West Publishing Company. It can be used alone, or in combination with other books in the series.

How to Use This Book

You should complete all six units, which will give you both the fundamentals of Basic programming and a solid foundation introduction to object programming with Visual Basic. These beginning units present the most commonly used Visual Basic controls and the three fundamental logic structures—sequence, loop, and decision. You will learn that these three structures are the only structures required to write any program. Do as much work on the computer as you can by completing the Guided Activities and as many program Exercises as possible. There is no better way to learn to program than sitting down at the computer and trying things for yourself.

Each unit contains the following features:

LEARNING OBJECTIVES The knowledge and skills addressed in the unit.

IMPORTANT VISUAL BASIC KEYWORDS The keywords to be covered, which will later serve as a quick reference for the statements presented in the unit.

GUIDED ACTIVITIES Step-by-step, hands-on computer activities designed to show how various aspects of the Visual Basic environment operate (such as setting control properties), to further illustrate certain keywords, and to explore other programming techniques.

EXERCISES Computer programs for you to design, write, and test on your own. All exercises require you to follow good programming practices.

REVIEW QUESTIONS Questions designed to test your mastery of the material presented in a given unit. Answers to selected Review Questions are contained in Appendix A.

IMPORTANT TERMS A list of the important terms and concepts discussed in the unit. This list is designed to help review the unit.

Additional features of this book are as follows:

SCREEN CAPTURES Used to show you exactly what you should see on your computer screen at certain times.

INDEX The index covers functions, keywords, important terms, sample programs, statements, and other topics. It is designed to allow you to find relevant material quickly.

QUICK REFERENCE   This reference is placed at the back of the book, where you can easily refer to it.

THE WEST INSTRUCTOR SOLUTIONS DISK   This disk contains a solution to all of the programming exercises.

A Note of Thanks

- to Nancy Hill-Whilton of West Publishing for effective guidance in the development of the manuscript.

- to Labrecque Publishing Services, whose team of editors, accuracy checkers, input editors, page makeup specialists, and proofreaders turned the manuscript into the attractive book you are about to study.

- to the reviewers for their constructive criticism and many valuable suggestions.

This Book Is Dedicated . . .

- to Jessica, Kelly, Zachary, T. J., Tyler, and Tory, my grandchildren, who will someday read this book and learn to program.

Jonathan C. Barron
December, 1994

This book is part of THE MICROCOMPUTING SERIES. This popular series provides the most comprehensive list of books dealing with microcomputer applications software. We have expanded the number of software topics and provided a flexible set of instructional materials for all courses. This unique series includes five different types of books.

1. *West's Microcomputing Custom Editions* give instructors the power to create a spiral-bound microcomputer applications book especially for their course. Instructors can select the applications they want to teach and the amount of material they want to cover for each application—essentials or intermediate length. The following titles are available for the 1995 Microcomputing Series custom editions program:

Understanding Information Systems	*Lotus 1-2-3 Release 2.01*
Management, Information, and Systems:	*Lotus 1-2-3 Release 2.2*
An Introduction to Information Systems	*Lotus 1-2-3 Release 2.3*
Understanding Networks	*Lotus 1-2-3 Release 2.4*
DOS (3.x) and System	*Lotus 1-2-3 Release 3*
DOS 5 and System	*Lotus 1-2-3 for Windows Release 4*
DOS 6 and System	*Lotus 1-2-3 for Windows Release 5*
Microsoft Windows 3.0	*Microsoft Excel 3*
Microsoft Windows 3.1	*Microsoft Excel 4*
Microsoft Windows 95	*Microsoft Excel 5.0*
WordPerfect 5.0	*Quattro Pro 4*
WordPerfect 5.1	*Quattro Pro 5.0 for Windows*
WordPerfect 6.0	*Quattro Pro 6.0 for Windows*
WordPerfect for Windows (Release 5.1 and 5.2)	*dBASE III Plus*
	dBASE IV Version 1.0/1.1/1.5
WordPerfect 6.0 for Windows	*dBASE IV Version 2.0*
Microsoft Powerpoint 4.0	*Paradox 3.5*
Microsoft Word for Windows Version 1.1	*Paradox 4.5 for Windows*
Microsoft Word for Windows Version 2.0	*QBasic*
Microsoft Word for Windows Version 6.0	*Microsoft Visual Basic*
PageMaker 4	*Microsoft Access 1.1*
PageMaker 5.0	*Microsoft Access 2.0*

For more information about *West's Microcomputing Custom Editions*, please contact your local West Representative, or call West Publishing Company at 512-327-3175.

2. General concepts books for teaching basic hardware and software philosophy and applications are available separately or in combination with hands-on applications. These books provide students with a general overview of computer fundamentals including history, social issues, and a synopsis of software and hardware applications. These books include *Understanding Information Systems*, by Steven C. Ross, and *Management, Information, and Systems: An Introduction to Information Systems*, by William Davis.

3. A series of hands-on laboratory tutorials (*Understanding and Using*) are software specific and cover a wide range of individual packages. These tutorials, written at an introductory level, combine tutorials with complete reference guides. A complete list of series titles can be found on the following pages.

4. Several larger volumes combining DOS with three application software packages are available in different combinations. These texts are titled *Understanding and Using Application Software*. They condense components of the individual lab manuals and add conceptual coverage for courses that require both software tutorials and microcomputer concepts in a single volume.

5. A series of advanced-level, hands-on lab manuals provide students with a strong project/systems orientation. These include *Understanding and Using Lotus 1-2-3: Advanced Techniques Releases 2.2 and 2.3*, by Judith C. Simon.

THE MICROCOMPUTING SERIES has been successful in providing you with a full range of applications books to suit your individual needs. We remain committed to excellence in offering the widest variety of current software packages. In addition, we are committed to producing microcomputing texts that provide you both the coverage you desire and also the level and format most appropriate for your students. The Executive Editor of the series is Rick Leyh of West Educational Publishing; the Consulting Editor is Steve Ross of Western Washington University. We are always planning for the future in this series. Please send us your comments and suggestions:

Rick Leyh
West Educational Publishing
1515 Capital of Texas Highway South
Suite 402
Austin, TX 78746
Internet: RLEYH@RESEARCH.WESTLAW.COM

Steve Ross
Associate Professor/MIS
College of Business and Economics
Western Washington University
Bellingham, Washington 98225-9077
Internet: STEVEROSS@WWU.EDU

We now offer these books in THE MICROCOMPUTING SERIES:

General Concepts

Management, Information, and Systems: An Introduction to Information Systems
by William Davis

Understanding Information Systems
by Steven C. Ross

Understanding Computer Information Systems
by Paul W. Ross, H. Paul Haiduk, H. Willis Means, and Robert B. Sloger

Understanding and Using the Macintosh
by Barbara Zukin Heiman and Nancy E. McGauley

Operating Systems/Environments

Understanding and Using Microsoft Windows95
by Steven C. Ross and Ronald W. Maestas

Understanding and Using Microsoft Windows 3.1
by Steven C. Ross and Ronald W. Maestas

Understanding and Using Microsoft Windows 3.0
by Steven C. Ross and Ronald W. Maestas

Understanding and Using MS-DOS 6.0
by Jonathan P. Bacon

Understanding and Using MS-DOS/PC DOS 5.0
by Jonathan P. Bacon

Understanding and Using MS-DOS/PC DOS 4.0
by Jonathan P. Bacon

Networks

Understanding Networks
by E. Joseph Guay

Programming

Essentials of Microsoft Visual Basic
by Jonathan C. Barron

Understanding and Using QBasic
by Jonathan C. Barron

Word Processors

Understanding and Using WordPerfect 6.0 for Windows
by Jonathan P. Bacon

Understanding and Using WordPerfect for Windows
by Jonathan P. Bacon

Understanding and Using Microsoft Word for Windows 6.0
Emily M. Ketcham

Understanding and Using Microsoft Word for Windows 2.0
by Larry Lozuk and Emily M. Ketcham

Understanding and Using Microsoft Word for Windows (1.1)
by Larry Lozuk

Understanding and Using WordPerfect 6.0
by Jonathan P. Bacon and Robert G. Sindt

Understanding and Using WordPerfect 5.1
by Jonathan P. Bacon and Cody T. Copeland

Understanding and Using WordPerfect 5.0
by Patsy H. Lund

Desktop Publishing

Understanding and Using PageMaker 5.0
by John R. Nicholson

Understanding and Using PageMaker 4
by John R. Nicholson

Spreadsheet Software

Understanding and Using Microsoft Excel 5.0
by Steven C. Ross and Stephen V. Hutson

Understanding and Using Microsoft Excel 4
by Steven C. Ross and Stephen V. Hutson

Understanding and Using Microsoft Excel 3
by Steven C. Ross and Stephen V. Hutson

Understanding and Using Quattro Pro 6.0 for Windows
by Lisa Friedrichsen

Understanding and Using Quattro Pro 5.0 for Windows
by Larry D. Smith

Understanding and Using Quattro Pro 4
by Steven C. Ross and Stephen V. Hutson

Understanding and Using Lotus 1-2-3 Release 5
by Steven C. Ross and Dolores Pusins

Understanding and Using Lotus 1-2-3 for Windows Release 4
by Steven C. Ross and Dolores Pusins

Understanding and Using Lotus 1-2-3 Release 3
by Steven C. Ross

Understanding and Using Lotus 1-2-3 Release 2.3 and Release 2.4
by Steven C. Ross

Understanding and Using Lotus 1-2-3: Advanced Techniques Releases 2.2 and 2.3
by Judith C. Simon

Understanding and Using Lotus 1-2-3 Release 2.2
by Steven C. Ross

Understanding and Using Lotus 1-2-3 Release 2.01
by Steven C. Ross

Database Management Software

Understanding and Using Microsoft Access 2.0
by Bruce J. McLaren

Understanding and Using Microsoft Access 1.1
by Bruce J. McLaren

Understanding and Using Paradox 4.5 for Windows
by Larry D. Smith

Understanding and Using Paradox 3.5
by Larry D. Smith

Understanding and Using dBASE IV Version 2.0
by Steven C. Ross

Understanding and Using dBASE IV
by Steven C. Ross

Understanding and Using dBASE III Plus, 2nd Edition
by Steven C. Ross

Integrated Software

Understanding and Using Microsoft Works for Windows 3.0
by Gary Bitter

Understanding and Using Microsoft Works 3.0 for the PC
by Gary Bitter

Understanding and Using Microsoft Works 3.0 for the Macintosh
by Gary Bitter

Understanding and Using Microsoft Works 2.0 on the Macintosh
by Gary Bitter

Understanding and Using Microsoft Works 2.0 on the IBM PC
by Gary Bitter

Understanding and Using ClarisWorks
by Gary Bitter

Presentation Software

Understanding and Using Microsoft Powerpoint 4.0
by Karen Young

Combined Books

Essentials of Application Software, Volume 1: DOS, WordPerfect 5.0/5.1, Lotus 1-2-3 Release 2.2, dBASE III Plus
by Steven C. Ross, Jonathan P. Bacon, and Cody T. Copeland

Understanding and Using Application Software, Volume 4: DOS, WordPerfect 5.0, Lotus 1-2-3 Release 2, dBASE IV
by Patsy H. Lund, Jonathan P. Bacon, and Steven C. Ross

Understanding and Using Application Software, Volume 5: DOS, WordPerfect 5.0/5.1, Lotus 1-2-3 Release 2.2, dBASE III Plus
by Steven C. Ross, Jonathan P. Bacon, and Cody T. Copeland

Advanced Books

Understanding and Using Lotus 1-2-3: Advanced Techniques Releases 2.2 and 2.3
by Judith C. Simon

Jonathan C. Barron holds a B.A. degree in Mathematics from Rutgers, The State University of New Jersey; an M.S. degree in Applied Mathematics from Stevens Institute of Technology; and an M.A. degree in Mathematics from Bryn Mawr College. He has 33 years of teaching experience in mathematics and more than 20 years in teaching programming. For the past 24 years, he has been teaching mathematics and programming at Eastern College, St. Davids, Pennsylvania.

In the late 1970s, when microcomputers were making their debut, he was the assistant director of a two-year project to investigate the use of microcomputers in the small-college environment, sponsored by the National Science Foundation. At the end of this project, he served as the Chair of the Computer Science Department at Eastern College, St. Davids, Pennsylvania, until 1985. This experience led to a BASIC programming text published by Holt, Rinehart & Winston in 1983. *Understanding and Using QBasic* was published by West Publishing in the fall of 1994.

1 *Using the Computer*

This unit begins your study of the Visual Basic Programming System for Windows. Several fundamental statements are introduced to enable you to begin writing your own Visual Basic programs. The topics covered include how to create a user interface, write and enter program code, and execute and save a Visual Basic application.

Learning Objectives

At the completion of this unit you should know

1. how to write a simple Visual Basic application,

2. what objects, events, and projects are,

3. how to draw control objects such as command buttons, labels, text boxes, and picture boxes, and set their properties,

4. how to use the Print method,

5. what variables are and how they are stored,

6. how to document the program code using remarks,

7. what is meant by a sequence structure,

8. how a flowchart can be used to outline the steps of a procedure,

9. how to use the usual arithmetic operations to write arithmetic expressions in Visual Basic.

At the completion of this unit you should be able to

1. start Visual Basic,

2. create, enter, and run a simple Visual Basic application,

3. draw a Visual Basic user interface,

4. use the Toolbox and the toolbar,

5. print a hard copy of a project,

6. save a project on a disk,

7. use the Properties window,

8. exit Visual Basic.

Important Keywords

Cls

End

Let

Print

Rem

Sub

Using the Computer to Find Simple Interest

Learning to program is much like learning a foreign language. At the beginning, we learn the common words and their definitions. Later we learn to write and speak short sentences. At first, our writing and speaking are not elegant, but we manage to convey our ideas. As we become more at ease with the language and grow to more fully understand the meanings of words and phrases, our writing and conversation become more elegant and precise. Likewise, when learning a computer language we first learn simple commands that help us write instructions to the computer. The set of instructions (the program code) is often clumsy and longer than necessary, but it gets the job done. As we learn more about the "language" and how the computer translates code into action, our instructions become more efficient. Our goal is not just "to get the job done," but to get it done with a program that is well organized, readable, easy to modify, and reliable. In this text, we have chosen the Visual Basic Programming System to achieve this goal.

Computers solve problems just like we do. For example, if we want to find the simple interest on an investment of $1,000 at 10.534% per year for 7 years, we use the simple interest formula

Interest = (Principal)×(Annual Rate of Interest)×(Time in Years)

or

Interest = (Princ)(AnnRate)(TimeYr)

where Interest stands for the simple interest, Princ for the principal or the amount invested ($1000), AnnRate for the annual interest rate (expressed in decimal form as .10534), and TimeYr for the number of years the money is invested (7 years). Thus, substituting the values given into our formula, the result would be as follows:

I = (1000)(.10534)(7) = 737.38

To get the computer to make this computation, we write a set of instructions (code) that the computer can understand and execute using the Visual Basic programming language. The task that you want the computer to perform is called an **application**. In this case the application is finding the simple interest on an investment.

The Rem Statement

For this application, we begin the Visual Basic program code with a Rem statement to identify the application. Rem is short for "remark." Rem statements are used to provide information about the code. The first line of our code is

```
Rem Simple Interest Application #1
```

The word Rem indicates to the computer that the statement contains explanatory information and is to be ignored when the code is executed, that is, it is **nonexecutable**. You may write *anything* following Rem. In place of Rem, you may substitute an apostrophe ('). For instance, the first line of code could also be written as

```
' Simple Interest Application #1
```

The Let Statement

Next, the computer must be told the value of Princ. This is done by means of an **assignment statement**, called the Let statement, such as

```
Let Princ = 1000
```

The word Let is a command in Visual Basic that tells the computer to assign a certain value to a variable. In this case, it tells the computer to assign the value 1000 to the variable Princ. In general, a **variable** is a memory location used to store different values during the solution of a problem. There are four variables in this application: the principal (Princ), the interest rate (AnnRate), the time (TimeYr), and the interest (Interest). A variable is identified in code by a variable name that begins with a letter and can contain as many as 40 characters. The characters can be letters and/or numeric digits. However, certain combinations reserved for Visual Basic statements such as Let or Rem cannot be used as variable names. Later on you will learn that certain characters—namely, %, &, !, #, @, $—can be attached to variable names to determine what type of data can be stored in that variable. If none of these symbols is attached to the variable name, then Visual Basic automatically makes the variable a type called *Variant*. The Variant data type is capable of storing numeric, date/time, or string (character sequences) data.

The assignment statement uses the familiar symbol = (equal sign) to assign a value to a variable. To understand what it means to "assign a value," picture the computer's memory as being divided into cells much like a group of mailboxes in a post office, and think of a variable as a name for one of the cells. When a variable is assigned a value, the computer names, and stores a value in, one of these cells, as shown in Figure 1.1.

FIGURE 1.1
Memory cells

Cell name

Contents

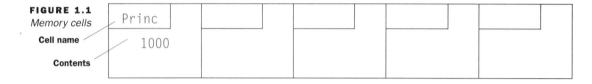

Thus,

```
Let Princ = 1000
```

causes the computer to name a *memory cell* Princ and store the number 1000 in this cell.

For the fourth and fifth lines we use the assignment statements

```
AnnRate = .10534
TimeYr = 7
```

NOTE *We have omitted the word Let, since Visual Basic does not require it. Visual Basic treats any statement containing an equal sign as an assignment statement.*

These lines cause the computer to store 0.10534 and 7 in memory cells named AnnRate and TimeYr, respectively, as shown in Figure 1.2.

FIGURE 1.2
Memory cells after the assignment statements are executed

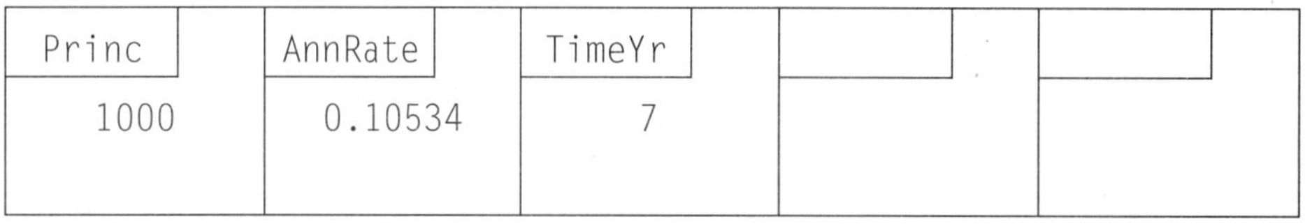

Princ	AnnRate	TimeYr		
1000	0.10534	7		

When reading these lines, it may be helpful to read the equal sign as "gets." Thus, the first line would be read as "Princ gets 1000," the second as "AnnRate gets .10534," and the third as "TimeYr gets 7."

After assigning the values of Princ, AnnRate, and TimeYr, the next task is to instruct the computer to compute the interest I—the product of Princ, AnnRate, and TimeYr. To find this product, we use the assignment statement

```
Interest = Princ * AnnRate * TimeYr
```

where * is used to indicate the operation of multiplication, that is, Interest gets the product of Princ, AnnRate, and TimeYr. Any arithmetic operation we want performed must be indicated between the variables. The computer interprets this line as "evaluate the formula on the right-hand side of the equal sign and assign (store) the resulting value to (in) the variable (memory cell) named on the left-hand side." Thus, when executed this line will cause the computer to compute the product of Princ, AnnRate, and TimeYr and store the result in the memory cell Interest, as shown in Figure 1.3.

FIGURE 1.3
Memory cells after execution of these lines

Princ	AnnRate	TimeYr	Interest	
1000	0.10534	7	737.38	

NOTE *No values are assigned or computed until the program is executed or "run" by the computer. When the computer runs these lines, everything takes place inside the computer.*

The Print Method

What is needed next is a command to instruct the computer to output the value of Interest in some designated area of the display screen (how to designate an area will be explained later). Visual Basic provides the ***Print method*** (a formal description of the Print method will be given later in this unit) for this purpose. For now, we use the following line to output the interest.

```
Print "The Interest is ", Interest
```

This line causes the computer to print

```
The Interest is          737.38
```

in a default window, called a *form*, when the lines are executed. Exactly what a form is will be made clear in our description of the Visual Basic programming environment and in the first Guided Activity.

The Print method instructs the computer to print

- The message within quotes, and

- The contents of memory cell Interest.

NOTE *The computer prints the contents of cell Interest, not the word "Interest." Any words to be printed literally must be contained within double quotation marks.*

Here is the complete code.

Simple Interest Application #1

```
Rem Simple Interest Application #1
Princ = 1000
AnnRate = .10534
TimeYr = 7
Interest = Princ * AnnRate * TimeYr
Print "The Interest is ", Interest
```

The next step in the development of our simple interest application is to learn how to enter our code into the computer and to create the user *interface*. We begin with an introduction to Visual Basic.

The Visual Basic Programming Environment

Visual Basic is started from Windows by double-clicking the Visual Basic icon in the Program Manager window. After a short delay, you will see the initial Visual Basic Programming Environment screen as shown in Figure 1.4.

FIGURE 1.4
The Visual Basic programming environment

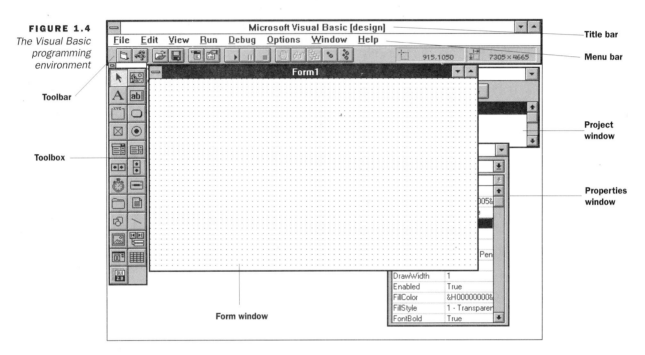

This screen is made up of the following elements.

Title Bar

The *title bar* is at the top of the screen and contains the name of the window (Microsoft Visual Basic [design]). On the left end of the title bar is the Window Control-menu box. On the right end are the Minimize and Maximize buttons.

Menu Bar

The *menu bar* contains a list of menu titles. Each menu title is activated by clicking its icon or by pressing [Alt] followed by the first letter of the title. Pressing [Esc] will cancel your selection. When activated, a drop-down menu appears containing a list of commands available under that title. These commands are used to help create your applications. Only the **bolded** commands are currently available for use.

Toolbar

The third line on the screen, shown in Figures 1.4 and 1.5, is called the *toolbar*. It contains 14 icons, or buttons representing commands used in the programming environment. These commands are executed by clicking the corresponding icon.

FIGURE 1.5
The Visual Basic toolbar

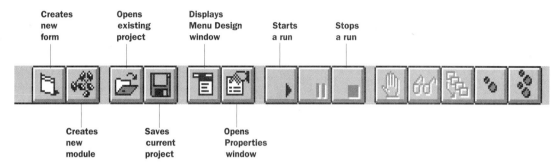

Table 1.1 gives a brief explanation of the four commands used in this unit. The others will be explained later when they are used.

TABLE 1.1
Action initiated by clicking certain toolbar icons

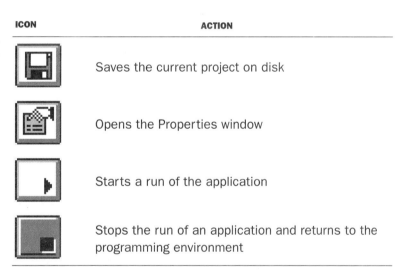

ICON	ACTION
	Saves the current project on disk
	Opens the Properties window
	Starts a run of the application
	Stops the run of an application and returns to the programming environment

Form

The form is the large stippled window in Figure 1.4 containing a title bar similar to the title bar described above. It is used to design the interface between your application and the user. It is used for both input to and output from your application, as we will see in the Guided Activities to follow.

Toolbox

The *Toolbox* contains 23 icons that represent *objects* called *controls* that can be placed on a form. Figure 1.6 shows the name of each control in the Toolbox. In this unit we will discuss text boxes, labels, command buttons, and picture boxes.

FIGURE 1.6
The Visual Basic Toolbox

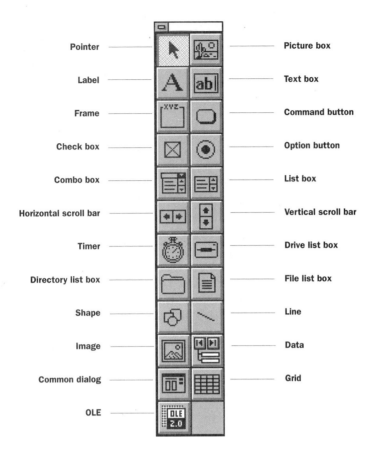

Pointer	Picture box
Label	Text box
Frame	Command button
Check box	Option button
Combo box	List box
Horizontal scroll bar	Vertical scroll bar
Timer	Drive list box
Directory list box	File list box
Shape	Line
Image	Data
Common dialog	Grid
OLE	

Project Window

The *Project window* is partially hidden behind the form window. When any portion of this window is clicked, the window shows a list of forms, code modules, and custom control files in the current project. A *project* is a collection of files containing the programming code and the user interface used to implement a Visual Basic application.

Properties Window

The *Properties window* is also partially hidden behind the form. It lists the *properties* and their *settings* for a selected object. The settings of the properties control the appearance and function of a given object. We will be learning about each of these properties as the need to know arises.

As you progress through the text, you will learn how to use the tools provided in the programming environment by working with them in the Guided Activities. Don't overly concern yourself if you feel a bit overwhelmed at this point. Visual Basic has many features and we'll try to present them slowly and carefully through "hands on" experience in the Guided Activities. To get started, complete Guided Activity 1.1.

GUIDED ACTIVITY 1.1

Creating, Running, and Saving a Visual Basic Application

Features of Visual Basic contained in this activity:

- Caption property
- Click event
- Code window
- Command button
- Form
- Properties window

In this activity we complete the development of our simple interest application by entering it into the computer and running it. In the process we must draw a user interface and show how code is entered. Several features of Visual Basic will have to be introduced and explained. You will also be shown how to save your project for future use.

1. Start Visual Basic from Windows by double-clicking the Visual Basic icon. The Visual Basic programming environment shown earlier in Figure 1.4 should be on your screen after a short delay, as the program is loaded into memory.

2. We begin programming the simple interest application by creating the user interface. Double-click the Command button in the Toolbox. It is the third icon in the right-hand column, a rounded rectangle. This puts a default-sized object called a *command button* captioned Command1 in the middle of the form as shown in Figure 1.7.

FIGURE 1.7
A command button showing sizing handles

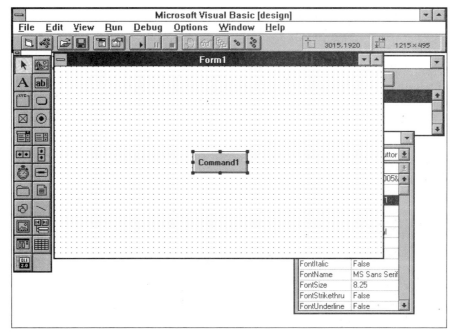

The small black rectangles in the corners and on the sides of this button are called *sizing handles*. They are used to change the size of the control as we will see in this activity.

3. Place the mouse arrow on this command button and *drag* it to rest on the third row of dots from the bottom of the form. To drag an object, press and hold the left mouse button down and move the object with the mouse.

4. Open the Properties window by clicking the Properties window icon (sixth icon from the left) on the toolbar or by pressing F4. Figure 1.8 shows the Properties window.

FIGURE 1.8
*Properties
window*

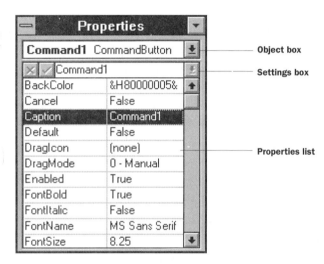

This window contains the following elements—an *Object box*, a *Settings box*, and a *Properties list*.

- Object box—This box displays the type and name of the object.

- Settings box—This box displays the setting for the highlighted property in the properties list. The setting may be edited using the same edit commands usually found in a text editor such as Edit in DOS or Notepad in Windows. If the arrow on the right of the box is bolded, then some settings can be changed by clicking this arrow to display a list of choices. A choice is selected by clicking on it.

- Properties list—All of the property choices for the object are displayed in the left column with the current setting for each shown in the right column.

5. Select the *Caption property* with the [↑] and [↓] keys or by clicking it with the mouse. If the Caption property is not visible in the window, use the vertical scroll bar or the [↑] and [↓] keys to bring it into view.

6. Type the caption Execute Code in the settings box. Notice that the caption appears inside the command button as you type.

7. Click anywhere on the form (except on the command button) or press [Alt] and [F4], simultaneously (symbolized by [Alt][F4]), to close the Properties window. Figure 1.9

FIGURE 1.9
Command button containing a caption

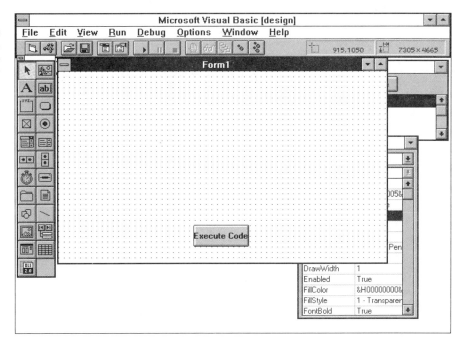

shows the result. Our caption looks a little cramped in this ***default-sized*** button (that is, the size of its initial setting).

8. Click anywhere inside the command button. This causes sizing handles to appear. When the sizing handles are present on a control, the control is called *active*. When they are missing it is called *inactive*.

9. Make the command button a little longer by dragging the sizing handle in the middle of the right side of the button a few dots to the right. Dragging means holding down the left mouse button while moving the object to a new location with the mouse. When the mouse pointer is placed on a sizing handle, the pointer switches to a double-headed arrow.

10. Next we enter the code. Double-click the command button on the form to open the ***Code window***. You can also open the Code window for an active object by pressing ⌨F7. Figure 1.10 shows what you will see next.

   Two features of this window are the ***Object box*** and the ***Procedure box*** (labeled Proc.), directly under the title bar of the Code window.

   ■ Object box—Shows the name of the selected object for coding purposes. The arrow on the right of this box is bolded if there are other objects attached to this form. A click on this arrow displays a list of these objects.

   ■ Procedure box—Clicking the arrow to the right of this box will display all of the procedures that can be associated with the object—in this case a command button. In this example, the procedure is called ***Click*** which refers to the ***event*** that will cause the code to be executed; that is, when the application is run and the user clicks the command button, the code associated with this button will be executed.

FIGURE 1.10
*The Code
window with
event procedure
template*

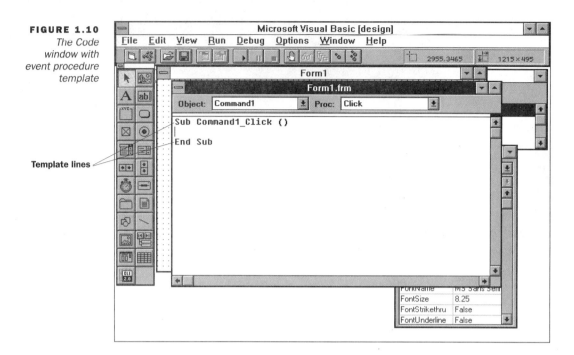

Template lines

11. Visual Basic automatically supplies the first and last line of the *event procedure* as a *template*. The first line gives the name of the procedure (Command1) and the type of event (a click with the mouse) that causes the procedure code to be executed. The cursor is a blinking vertical line between these two lines. The End Sub statement marks the end of the procedure. Type the first line of code we developed for the Simple Interest Application #1 shown here.

```
rem Simple Interest Application #1
```

Type the word `rem` using lowercase letters. Correct any errors with the [Backspace] key.

12. Press [Enter] at the end of the line to enter the line and open a new blank line. Visual Basic automatically converts the first letter of the word rem to uppercase and changes the color of the word to blue (if you are working with a color monitor). This helps you recognize reserved words in the code. Also, the text of all remarks are converted to green.

13. Continue entering the remaining five lines of code. When you are finished, your screen should look something like Figure 1.11.

    The End Sub statement indicates the logical end of the procedure. It terminates the execution of the procedure.

14. To start the application, click the Start run icon on the toolbar or press [F5]. Figure 1.12 shows you the next screen.

15. Now, click the Execute Code button on the form or press [Enter]. The output appears in the upper-left corner of the form as shown in Figure 1.13.

FIGURE 1.11
Code window with program code

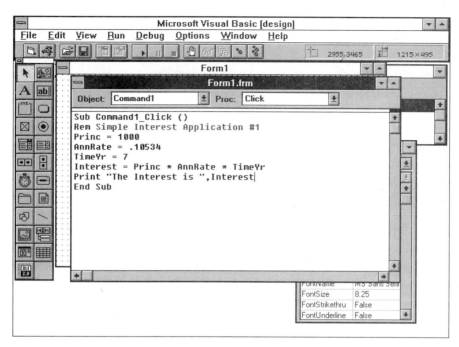

FIGURE 1.12
Form at start of run

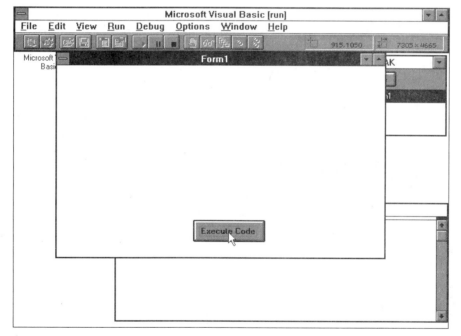

NOTE *Unless coded otherwise (additional coding options will be covered later), the Print method prints to the current form.*

16. To stop the run of the application, click the Stop run icon (the ninth from the left) on the toolbar or open the Run menu and select End.

FIGURE 1.13

*Form showing
output after
clicking the
Execute Code
button*

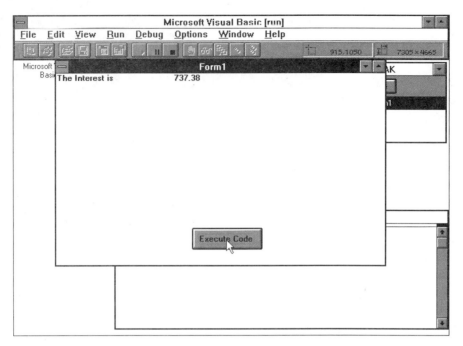

17.   Click the Save project icon (looks like a 3.5" disk) on the toolbar to save the project. Figure 1.14 shows the Save File As dialog box that pops up on the screen. Type `sminap#1` (see note below) in the File Name box and click OK.

Visual Basic automatically adds the file extension .frm to the file name.

FIGURE 1.14

*The Save File As
dialog box*

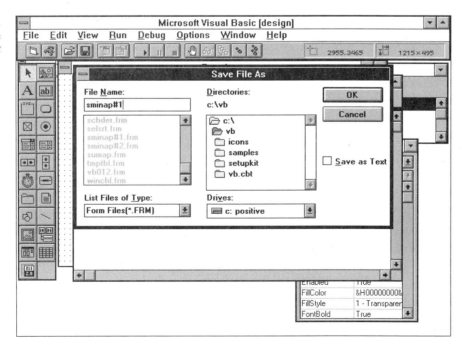

NOTE *Before saving your project, check with your instructor. You may be instructed to save your work on your own personal floppy disk. In that case, you should include the name of the appropriate drive as part of the file name, such as* a:sminap#1.

18. The next screen that appears is called the Save Project As dialog box and is shown in Figure 1.15. Type the same name as in step 17 in the File Name box and click OK. Visual Basic adds the extension .mak to the name. This file holds a list of all of the files associated with the current project.

FIGURE 1.15
The Save Project As dialog box

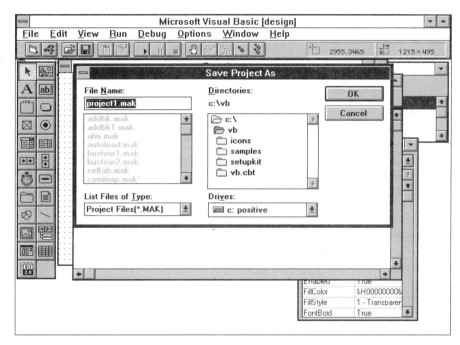

19. To exit Visual Basic, click Exit from the drop-down menu under the File title on the menu bar.

CAUTION *To avoid data loss, always exit Visual Basic and your applications in the approved manner. Never simply turn off the computer when an application is running.*

Sequence Structure

Let's examine the **structure** of the event procedure Command1_Click. It uses one of the three fundamental **control structures** known as the **sequence structure**. The other two are the **decision structure** and the **loop structure**. These structures are the building blocks of the **structured approach** to programming supported by Visual Basic. It can be shown that all program code can be written using only these three control structures.

The sequence structure is a sequence of program statements that are executed in order, one after the other, without any interruption or repetition. Diagramatically, it looks like Figure 1.16.

Flowcharts

Figure 1.16 is a *flowchart* for a sequence structure consisting of three blocks of statements. The number of statements included in a block is arbitrary. A flowchart is a symbolic outline, or "blueprint," of a procedure and is a useful device for understanding its logical structure. In a flowchart, a rectangular block is called a ***process block*** since it indicates some activity by the computer. The statements in block #1 are executed first, then those in block #2 followed by those in block #3. Control flows from statement block to statement block without interruption. Table 1.2 lists several other flowchart symbols we will be using throughout the text.

Figure 1.17 shows a flowchart for Command1_Click.

NOTE *We used the parallelogram to indicate the output of the value of the interest.*

Before continuing our study of programming, we will take some time to explain command buttons in more detail and introduce the ***text box***, the ***picture box***, and the ***label*** control objects.

FIGURE 1.16
A flowchart for the sequence structure

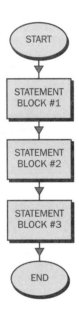

FIGURE 1.17
A flowchart for Command1_Click event procedure

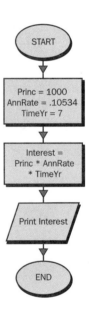

GUIDED ACTIVITY 1.2

Exploring Command Buttons

In this activity we work with command buttons. You are asked to draw one directly by dragging a cross hair and to resize it using the resizing handles.

1. Start Visual Basic from Windows by double-clicking the Visual Basic icon.

2. Click the Command button icon in the Toolbox.

3. Move the mouse pointer to the form, where it becomes a cross hair as shown in Figure 1.18.

TABLE 1.2
Standard flowchart symbols

SYMBOL	PURPOSE
⬭	The oval marks the start or the end of a flowchart.
▭	The rectangle is called a process block. It is used to show such things as computations and variable assignments.
▱	The parallelogram is called an input/output block and is used to show data either coming into or going out of the computer.
◇	The diamond is called a decision block and is used whenever the computer is required to make a decision as to what the next step is in the program. We'll use this symbol in Unit 5.
→	The arrow or flowline is used to show the direction of flow in the flowchart.
◯	The circle is used to connect separated sections of a flowchart.
▯	This block represents a code module containing a general procedure designed to accomplish a particular task. It is called when needed by other procedures.

4. Move the cross hair to the dot on the form where you want the upper-left corner of the command button to begin. Press and hold down the left mouse button.

5. Drag the cross hair across and down to the dot where you want the lower-right corner of the command button to end. Release the mouse button.

6. Click the Properties button on the toolbar.

7. Click on the Caption property (if it is not already highlighted) and type Cancel. As you type, the letters appear in the setting box and on the command button itself. To accept the caption, click the box containing a check mark on the settings box. To reject the caption, click the box with the X inside.

8. Close the Properties window.

CHECKPOINT 1A How do you close the Properties window?
The answers to checkpoint questions are contained in Appendix A.

9. Let's add another command button to the form. Double-click on the Command button icon in the Toolbox. This puts a default-sized command button in the center of the form with eight sizing handles.

10. Click the Properties window button on the toolbar.

FIGURE 1.18
*Shows
command
button cross hair*

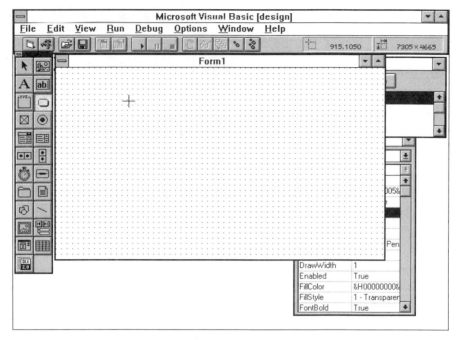

11. Click on the Caption property (if necessary).

12. Type `Push to Continue`. Notice that this phrase is too long for the default-sized button.

13. Place the mouse pointer on a sizing handle and drag the handle until the button is large enough to accommodate the phrase. Release the mouse button. A corner handle resizes controls both horizontally and vertically at the same time when dragged on a diagonal. A side handle resizes only horizontally, and a top or bottom handle resizes vertically.

14. Exit Visual Basic by clicking File on the menu bar and selecting Exit from the drop-down menu. There is no need to save anything, since we have only been experimenting, so answer no to any queries about saving.

GUIDED ACTIVITY 1.3

Exploring Text Boxes

New features of Visual Basic contained in this activity:

- Text boxes
- Text property

The objective of this activity is to introduce text box controls and to show how text may be written in them by the user.

1. Start Visual Basic from Windows by double-clicking the Visual Basic icon.

FIGURE 1.19
*Text box with
sizing handles*

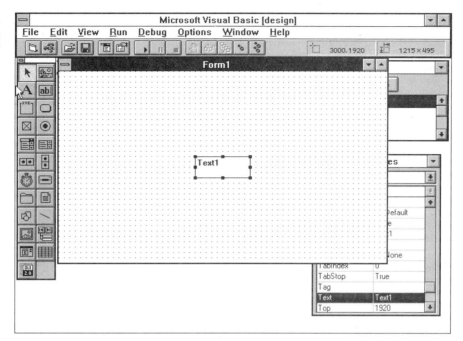

2. Double-click the Text box icon in the Toolbox (it is the second icon down in the right column of the Toolbox). A default-sized text box, with eight sizing handles, appears in roughly the center of the form as shown in Figure 1.19.

3. Click anywhere on the form outside of the text box to remove the sizing handles.

4. Click on the text box to restore the sizing handles.

5. Press Del to remove the text box.

6. Click the Edit title on the menu bar.

7. Click the Undo command to restore the text box on the form.

8. Click the Properties window icon on the toolbar to open the Properties window. In the Object box you will see Text1 in boldface followed by TextBox. Text1 is the current name of the text box and could be used to refer to this box in code.

9. Select the *Text property* from the properties list below the Settings box. This property is automatically selected by Visual Basic when the box is created, and the current value of the Text property is shown in the settings box. At the moment, a single default word Text1, highlighted in the Settings box, is the current value of the Text property. You can delete the current text by pressing the Backspace key.

10. Type your full name. Whatever you type replaces the word Text1 in the text box on the form and in the Settings box.

NOTE *The Settings box behaves like a standard text editor. That is, any text you enter can be edited by using the usual methods with which you are familiar. As a reminder, here are some of the editing commands.*

■ Del *erases the character immediately to the right of the cursor or any highlighted text.*

- Backspace erases the character immediately to the left of the cursor.

- Home moves the cursor to the start of the line.

- End moves the cursor to the end of the line.

- Ins switches between the Insert mode and the Overwrite mode.

11. Resize the text box to approximately 3 inches wide. Do not change the height.

12. Click the Properties icon and select the Text property again.

13. Place the cursor at the beginning of your name in the Settings box by placing the mouse pointer at the start of your name and clicking.

14. Type Mr. and Mrs. and watch how the letters are inserted in front of your name, as they would be in most word processors or text editors in the Insert mode.

15. Press End. The cursor jumps to the end of your name.

16. Type 7548 Sunset Drive, Anywhere, Any State, USA 19458. Eventually, your typing scrolls when you reach the end of the text box. It does *not* wrap to a new line.

17. Click the *Multiline property* in the properties list.

18. Click the arrow at the end of the Settings box and select True with the mouse.

19. Click on the text box on the form.

20. Resize the width just enough to see what you entered in step 16.

CHECKPOINT 1B   How do you resize an object?

21. Click the Run icon on the toolbar. The dots on the form disappear and the cursor is placed in the upper-left corner of the text box at the start of the text you entered in the above steps.

22. Press End. The cursor jumps to the end of the line.

23. Move the cursor to the end of the text by pressing Ctrl End and press Enter.

24. Type Joe Doaks.

25. Press Enter. Notice that the text scrolls upward.

26. Type 123 State Street.

27. Press Enter.

28. Type Camden, N.J.

29. Press Enter.

30. By now your name has scrolled out of view. Press Ctrl Home. Now your name, etc., should be visible.

31. Highlight your zip code in the text box.

32. Type 12345 to change your zip code. Basically, the text box behaves like a miniature word processor within the form.

33. Click the End icon to stop the run.

34. Exit Visual Basic without saving.

Exploring Picture Boxes and Labels

New features of Visual Basic contained in this activity:

- Alignment property
- AutoSize property
- BorderStyle property
- Labels
- Picture boxes
- Picture property

In this activity, we create a picture box and two labels that we'll use in the next sample application.

1. Start Visual Basic.

2. Click on the Picture box icon in the Toolbox (the first icon in the right column).

3. Move the mouse to the form and place the cross hair on the form about two-thirds of the way from the top of the form. Remember, you can go back later to move or resize this box at any time, so don't worry about the exact position when placing controls on the form.

4. Drag the cross hair diagonally down to the lower-right corner of the form.

5. Release the mouse. A picture box can be used to display a picture or text. We intend to display the output from our next application in a picture box.

6. Click on the Properties icon on the toolbar.

7. Double-click on the *Picture property* so that the Load Picture dialog box shown in Figure 1.20 appears.

8. Double-click on the root directory (c:\).

9. Select the Windows directory to see a list of pictures stored in the Windows directory as files with the .bmp (for "bitmap") extension.

10. Click OK.

11. Click on the winlogo.bmp file and click OK.

12. Activate the picture box (if necessary).

FIGURE 1.20
*Load Picture
dialog box*

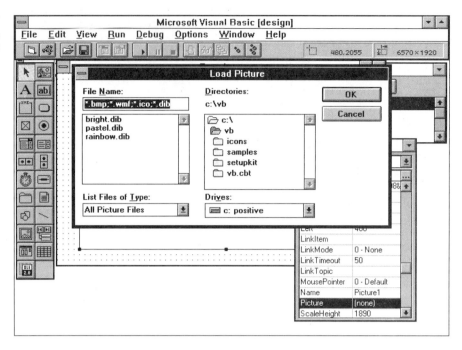

CHECKPOINT 1C   How do you activate an object?

13. Resize the picture box to match Figure 1.21.

14. Press [Del] to delete the picture box.

15. Double-click the Label icon in the Toolbox (the second icon in the left column). A default-sized label appears in the center of the form. The name of this label is Label1.

FIGURE 1.21
*Picture box
containing
Windows logo*

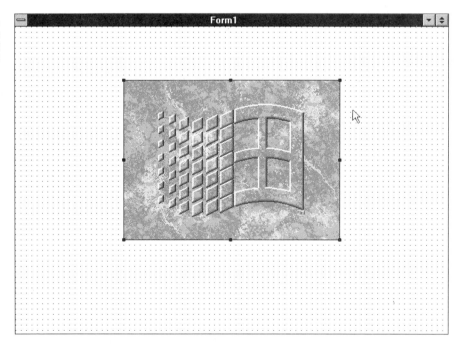

16. Click on the Properties icon on the toolbar or press [F4].

17. Click the Caption property (if necessary) and type `Principal` in the Settings box (that is, just start typing). A label provides text on a form that cannot be altered by the user.

18. Drag the label to about ½ inch from the top of the form and about ½ inch from the left edge of the form. Release the mouse button.

19. Resize the label to just one line.

20. Double-click the Label icon to add a second label, called Label2, to the form. Visual Basic automatically increments the number in the label name as each new label is added to the form.

21. Resize Label2 to just one line.

22. Click on the Properties icon on the Toolbox.

23. Click on the *AutoSize property* in the properties list.

24. Click the arrow at the end of the Settings box and click on the True option or press [T]. This allows the label to adjust automatically to accommodate captions too large for the current label size.

25. Click the Caption property in the properties list.

26. Change the caption to `Annual Rate in Decimal`, as you did in step 17.

27. Drag this second label to a position just below the first label.

28. Activate Label1 by clicking on it.

29. Click the Properties icon on the toolbar.

30. Click on the *Alignment property*.

31. Click on the arrow box on the right side of the Settings box. Note the three choices.

32. Click on each choice and watch the caption shift—from 0-Left Justify, to 1-Right Justify, to 2-Center. Leave the label right-justified.

33. Click the *BorderStyle property* in the properties list.

34. Click the arrow box on the Settings box.

35. Select 1-Fixed Single. This selection puts a box around your label.

36. Exit Visual Basic without saving anything.

Another Simple Interest Application

To solve a different simple interest problem using our first application, we would need to modify the code associated with the command button. This is very inconvenient and inefficient. A much better way is to redesign the user interface so that the user may enter the principal, the annual rate, and the time from the keyboard while the application is running. With this design, the interest can be computed on as many investments as the user desires.

We begin with a list of control objects for the interface. Since we want the user to be able to enter any values for the three variables, Princ, AnnRate, and TimeYr, we'll use three text boxes to receive these values together with three labels to prompt the user as to what value is entered in which text box. For the output display, we'll use a picture box. Two command buttons will be needed—one to execute the code after the user inputs the three variables, and another to exit properly from the application.

Figure 1.22 shows the initial design for the interface using default settings for all properties and objects.

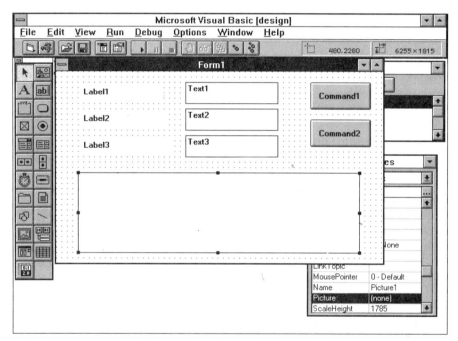

FIGURE 1.22
Initial design of the interface for the simple interest application

Next, we construct Table 1.3, listing the objects and the properties that need to be changed.

Two new properties are mentioned in the above table. The first is the ***WindowState property*** of the form. When we set this property to 2-Maximized, the form will fill the entire display screen when the application is run. The second is the ***Name property*** for the text boxes, the picture box, and the command buttons. When these objects are created, Visual Basic gives the Name property a default value. In the case of text boxes, the default value is Textn, where n is 1, 2, and 3. Visual Basic automatically increments n by 1 as each new text box is added to the form. The picture box gets the default name of Picture1, the command buttons get the default names Command1 and Command2, and the labels get the names Label1, Label2, and Label3.

There is no reason the default names cannot be used in the application. In fact we use them for the form and the labels. However, we change the names of the text boxes, the picture box, and the command buttons. Good programming habits dictate that we use a name more descriptive of the role the object plays in the application. In

TABLE 1.3
Objects and property settings for Simple Interest Application

OBJECT	PROPERTY	SETTING
Form1	Caption	Simple Interest Application
	WindowState	2-Maximized
Label1	Alignment	1-Right Justify
	Caption	Principal
Label2	Alignment	1-Right Justify
	AutoSize	True
	Caption	Annual Rate in Decimal
Label3	Alignment	1-Right Justify
	Caption	Time in Years
Text1	Name	txtPrinc
	Text	(blank)
Text2	Name	txtAnnRate
	Text	(blank)
Text3	Name	txtTimeYr
	Text	(blank)
Picture1	Name	picAppOutput
Command1	Caption	Execute
	Name	cmdExecute
Command2	Caption	Exit
	Name	cmdExit

this text, we will follow the naming conventions suggested by Microsoft in the Visual Basic *Programmer's Guide* shown in Table 1.4. The choices for our current application are shown in Table 1.3.

Our next task is to develop the code for the Execute command button.

Program Documentation

Documentation is a very important part of programming. As our applications become longer and more complex, good documentation becomes essential in order for us (and the intended users) to understand how the various procedures work. A *variable list* is a handy reference for those who read your code. After putting a project aside for a while, even the programmer can forget what variables stand for or the purpose of some statements. Thus, to develop good programming habits from the beginning, we document the code with a variable list and some explanatory remarks.

When the application is run, the user enters the three variables—Princ, AnnRate, and TimeYr—by typing their respective values in the appropriate text box. When a value is typed it is received into the computer as a *literal* string of characters, not as a

OBJECT	PREFIX	EXAMPLE
Check box	chk	chkSend
Combo box	cbo	cboLanguage
Command button	cmd	cmdExit
Data	dat	datAccount
Directory list box	dir	dirDestination
Drive list box	drv	drvSource
File list box	fil	filDiskA
Form	frm	frmMyForm
Frame	fra	fraButtons
Horizontal scroll bar	hsb	hsbProperties
Image	img	imgSnap
Label	lbl	lblInputNum
Line	lin	linEdge
List box	lst	lstSlate
Menu	mnu	mnuLunch
Option button	opt	optAMFM
Picture box	pic	picOutput
Shape	shp	shpOval
Text box	txt	txtAnnRate
Vertical scroll bar	vsb	vsbAccNums

TABLE 1.4 *Object naming conventions for Visual Basic*

number. They are stored as text in the Text property variables called txtPrinc.Text, txtAnnRate.Text, and txtTimeYr.Text, respectively. However, by default they are Variant variables and will be automatically converted to their equivalent numeric value by Visual Basic in any numeric expression or assignment statement. For example, if txtPrinc.Text = "1000", then Princ = txtPrinc.Text will assign the value 1000 to Princ.

In general, the contents of a text box are stored in the Text property that can be accessed in code by specifying the name of the text box followed by .Text. The correct syntax is

*textboxname.*Text

To enhance the application, we also compute the future value of the investment by adding the principal and interest together and outputting the result along with the interest.

Visual Basic Methods

A *method* is a built-in procedure supplied by Visual Basic and designed to carry out certain commands, such as printing, on objects. The syntax to call a method is as follows:

object.method

When executed, the computer applies the procedure called *method* to the *object*.

To illustrate, we'll use the **Cls method** to clear the picture box before printing the output in our current application.

The Cls Method—Syntax

[*object.*]Cls

The *object* refers to a form or a picture box. Cls clears any text or graphic images from the object. The square brackets around *object* mean it can be omitted when the current form is to be cleared. For our current application we use the following line:

```
picAppOutput.Cls
```

The output for the application is directed to the picture box using the Print method described here.

The Print Method—Syntax

[*object.*]Print [*expressionlist*]

The *object* refers to a form or picture box on which the *expressionlist* is to be printed. In this case it is a picture box and the appropriate lines of code are as follows:

```
picAppOutput.Print "The Interest is ", Interest
picAppOutput.Print "The Future Value of this Investment is ", FutVal
```

The complete code for the command buttons is shown next.

Code for the Execute Procedure

```
Sub cmdExecute_Click ()
Rem Variable List:
Rem   Princ = Principal
Rem   AnnRate = Annual Interest Rate
Rem   TimeYr = Time in Years
Rem   Interest = Simple Interest
Rem   FutVal = Future Value
Rem Retrieve values of variables from the text boxes
      Princ = txtPrinc.Text
      AnnRate = txtAnnRate.Text
      TimeYr = txtTimeYr.Text
Rem Compute the interest and the future value
```

```
            Interest = Princ * AnnRate * TimeYr
            FutVal = Interest + Princ
    Rem Print the results
            picAppOutput.Cls
            picAppOutput.Print "The Interest is ", Interest
            picAppOutput.Print "The Future Value is ", FutVal
    End Sub
```

Code for the Exit Procedure

```
    Sub cmdExit_Click ()
    Rem This procedure stops the run
            End
    End Sub
```

The *End statement* terminates the run of an application and is equivalent to clicking the Stop icon on the toolbar.

NOTE *To provide the user with a convenient way to exit a program correctly, an Exit command button should be included in all of your programs.*

GUIDED ACTIVITY 1.5

Entering and Running Simple Interest Application #2

New features of Visual Basic contained in this activity:

- Cls method

- End statement

- Exit button

- Name property

- WindowState property

In this activity we enter and run the Simple Interest Application #2. In the process we introduce some new Visual Basic statements and control properties.

1. Start Visual Basic.

2. Set the properties for the Form1 given in Table 1.3.

3. Create Label1 by double-clicking the Label icon in the Toolbox.

4. Move Label1 to the position shown in Figure 1.22.

CHECKPOINT 1D How do you reposition an object on a form?

5. Repeat steps 3 and 4 for Label2 and Label3.

6. Create, position, and resize the three text boxes shown in Figure 1.22.

7. Create and position the two command buttons shown in Figure 1.22.

8. Create a picture box by double-clicking the Picture box icon.

9. Position and resize the picture box to approximately the size shown in Figure 1.22 and set the Name property to `picAppOutput`.

10. Click on Label2 and set the Alignment and AutoSize properties according to Table 1.3. We do Label2 first since it has the longest caption.

11. Change the caption to the one given in Table 1.3.

12. Repeat steps 10 and 11 for Label1 and Label3.

13. Click on text box Text1.

14. Click the Properties icon on the toolbar.

15. Click on the Text property.

16. Press [Del] to clear the setting.

17. Click on the Name property.

18. Type the new Name as given in Table 1.3.

19. Repeat steps 13 through 18 for each of the other two text boxes.

20. Click the Command1 button.

21. Open the Properties window.

22. Set the Caption property according to Table 1.3.

CHECKPOINT 1E How do you change the Caption property?

23. Set the Name property according to Table 1.3.

24. Repeat steps 20 through 23 for the Command2 button. Figure 1.23 shows how the user interface form should appear at the end of step 24.

25. Double-click the Execute button to open the Code window.

NOTE *The object box contains the name cmdExecute in place of the default name. The same is true for the Sub statement on the template.*

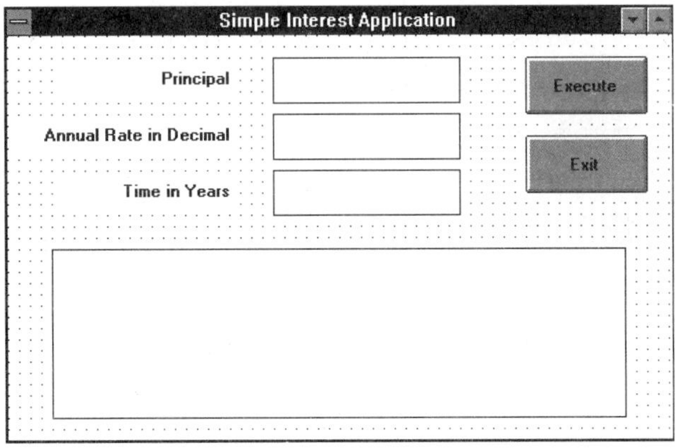

FIGURE 1.23
User interface after completing step 24 of Guided Activity 1.5

Simple Interest Application

Principal

Annual Rate in Decimal

Time in Years

Execute

Exit

26. Type in the code. When finished, click the arrow button on the object box and select cmdExit.

27. Enter the code for the Exit event procedure.

28. Click the Run icon on the toolbar.

29. Figure 1.24 shows how the user interface will appear to the user.

NOTE *If you entered the controls in the order given, the cursor should be blinking in the shape of an I-bar in the first text box labeled Principal. In Visual Basic this means that this text box has the* **focus**, *that is, it is active. If not, click this text box to give it the focus.*

FIGURE 1.24
User interface at start of run
Cursor

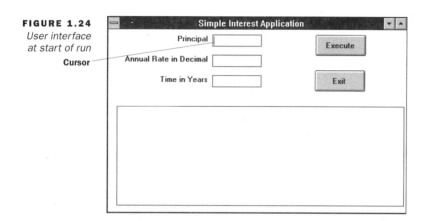

30. Type 2500 in this box and press ⎄Tab⎄ to advance to the next box, which gives the second text box the focus. If the second text box does not have the focus, keep pressing ⎄Tab⎄ until it does.

NOTE *Pressing* ⎄Tab⎄ *is the standard way to move from control to control on a form.*

31. Enter .065 in this box and press ⎄Tab⎄ to advance to the next text box.

32. Enter .25 in this box and press ⎄Tab⎄.

NOTE *The focus has moved to the Execute command button as indicated by the broken rectangle enclosing the word* Execute.

33. To see the output, either press ⎄Enter⎄ or click the Execute command button. The reason merely pressing ⎄Enter⎄ works is that the command button has the focus. Figure 1.25 shows what you will see next on the screen.

34. To change any of the values, click on the corresponding text box, highlight the current contents of the box, and type a new value. Try changing the annual rate to .12.

35. Click on the Execute button to see the new output.

36. To end the run, click on the Exit button. Visual Basic returns to the programming environment.

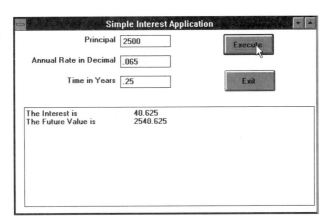

FIGURE 1.25
The form after clicking the Execute button

37. To obtain a hard copy of this application, click the File title on the menu bar.

38. Click Print on the drop-down file menu. The dialog box shown in Figure 1.26 appears.

Here is an explanation of the items in this box.

Option	Description
Current	Prints the active form or the code in the active Code window.
All	Prints all forms or all code in your application.
Form	Prints the current form or all forms in your application.
Form Text	Prints the text representation for the current form or all forms in your application. Use this feature to print out all form and control properties and their values.
Code	Prints the code for the current file or for all forms and modules in your application.
OK	Prints your selection.
Cancel	Closes the dialog box without printing.

FIGURE 1.26
Dialog box for Print command

39. The default setting is Current. Do not change this setting. Click the Form box, the Form Text box, and the Code box. This way you will get a complete copy of the project.

40. Click OK.

41. Save the project as sminap#2.

CHECKPOINT 1F   How do you save a project?

42.   Exit Visual Basic.

Keyword Syntax Review

Keyword—Syntax	Purpose
End	To terminate the run of a program
End Sub	To mark the end of a procedure. To terminate the execution of a procedure.
[object.]Cls	To clear any text or graphics from the given object
[Let] variable name = valueexpression	To assign values to variables
[object.]Print [expressionlist]	To print output on the given object
Rem any words of documentation or ' any words of documentation	To provide program documentation
Sub procedurename_event	To mark the beginning of a procedure

EXERCISE 1.1

Forms

Start Visual Basic and complete the following exercises.

1.   Change the Caption property on the form to My First Application.

2.   Change the Name property to frmMyForm.

3.   Set the WindowState property to 2-Maximized.

4.   Click the Run icon on the toolbar and observe carefully what happens.

5.   Click the Minimize button in the upper-right corner of the window and then click the Stop icon on the toolbar.

6.   Exit Visual Basic without saving anything.

EXERCISE 1.2

Command Buttons

Start Visual Basic and complete the following exercises.

1. Create a command button containing the words PUSH ME in bold print.

2. Change the FontItalic property to True.

3. Change the FontName property to New Times Roman.

4. Experiment with the FontSize property and observe what happens carefully.

5. Set the Name property to cmdPush.

6. Create another command button.

7. Set the Caption on this new button to EXIT PLEASE.

8. Experiment with resizing both command buttons. Pay close attention to what happens to the captions as you vary the size.

9. Click the Run icon on the toolbar. Press [Tab] several times and observe how the focus switches back and forth between the two buttons.

10. Click the Stop icon.

11. Exit Visual Basic without saving anything.

EXERCISE 1.3

Use (val) addn with text boxes.

Labels

Start Visual Basic and complete the following exercises.

1. Create a label on the form.

2. Set the AutoSize property to True.

3. Change the caption on the label to This Button is a Dummy.

4. Place a command button next to the label.

5. Create another label on the form.

6. Change the caption to Flintstone.

7. Set the Alignment property to 1-Right Justify.

8. Set the Alignment property to 2-Center.

9. Create a label containing your name in large bold italic letters.

10. Change the border on the label created in part 9 by setting the Border property.

11. Exit Visual Basic without saving.

EXERCISE 1.4

Text Boxes and Command Buttons

Start Visual Basic and complete the following exercises.

1. Create a text box containing the sentence If I have seen further it is by standing on the shoulders of Giants—Isaac Newton (1676).

2. Set the MultiLine property to True for the text box of part 1 and resize the box to show the quote.

3. Create a command button on the same form with the caption OK.

4. Create code for the command button of part 3 that writes Hello in the text box of part 1.

5. Exit Visual Basic without saving.

EXERCISE 1.5

Creating Miscellaneous Control Objects

1. Create a label with the word Check right-justified and italicized.

2. Create a label with the word Deposit right-justified and italicized.

3. Line up the two labels created in parts 1 and 2 in the upper-left corner.

4. Write the word Proverb in the title bar of the form.

5. Create a picture box on the form. Draw a command button on the form.

6. Enter code for the Click procedure of this command button to print the following quote in the picture box.

   ```
   "For since the fabric of the universe is
   most perfect and the work of a most
   wise Creator, nothing at all takes
   place in the universe in which some
   rule of maximum or minimum does
   not appear—Leonhard Euler"
   ```

7. Create a text box containing your name and address on three lines.

8. Exit Visual Basic without saving.

EXERCISE 1.6

License Application Form

Create a user interface for a driver's license application as shown in Figure 1.27 using labels, command buttons, and text boxes.

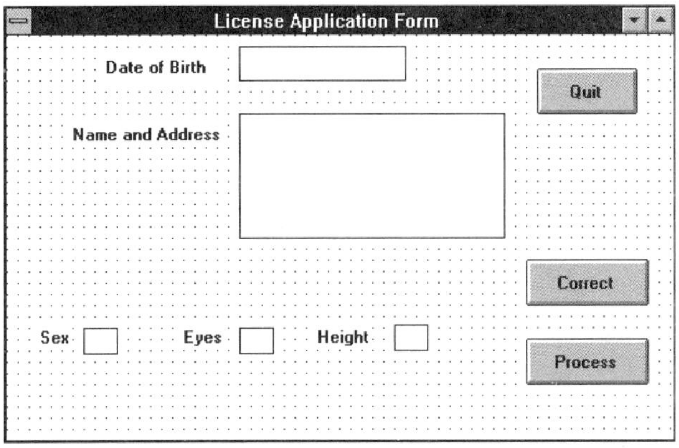

FIGURE 1.27
License application form

EXERCISE 1.7

Check Form

Create a user interface for writing a check as shown in Figure 1.28 using labels and text boxes.

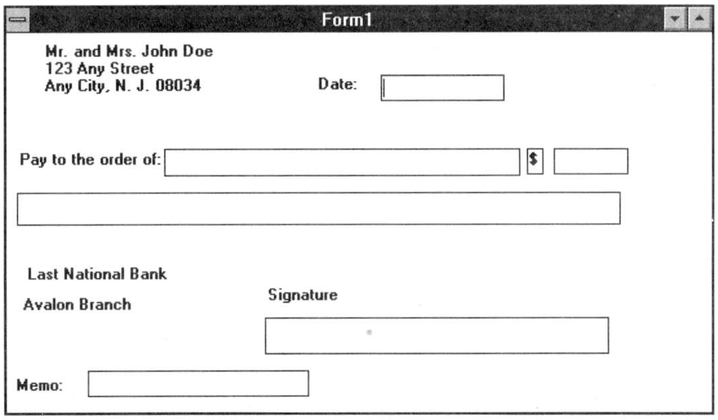

FIGURE 1.28
Check writing form

EXERCISE 1.8

Interest Rate for a Simple Interest Loan

Using sminap#2 as a model, create an application (interface and procedures) to find the annual rate, given the principal, the time, and the interest. Use the formula

```
AnnRate = Interest / (Princ * TimeYr)
```

Have the computer print the answer as a percent. Test the program using Interest = 62.5, Princ = 1250, and TimeYr = 5 years. The output should be AnnRate = .01 or 1%.

EXERCISE 1.9

Time for a Simple Interest Loan

Using sminap#2 as a model, create an application to find the time, given the principal, the annual rate, and the interest. Use the formula

```
TimeYr = Interest / (Princ * AnnRate)
```

EXERCISE 1.10

Principal for a Simple Interest Loan

Using sminap#2 as a model, create an application to find the principal, given the interest, the annual rate, and the time. Use the formula

```
Princ = Interest / (AnnRate * TimeYr)
```

Review Questions

The answers to questions marked with an asterisk are contained in Appendix A.

*1. Assuming that T = 0, A = 15, and B = 30, fill in the memory cells below using the following three lines:

```
Let T = A
Let A = B
Let B = T
```

After the first line has been executed, we have

T	A	B
115	2)5	30

After the second line has been executed, we have

T	A	B
15	30	30

After the third line has been executed, we have

T	A	B
15	30	15

What do these lines accomplish?

2. What is the purpose of the following Let statement?

```
Let X = -X
```

*3.   Is the following statement valid? If so, what is its purpose?

```
Let N = N + 1
```

*4.   Suppose that the following values are stored in memory.

A	B	C	D	S	T
0	36	9	10	25	0

Show the contents of these memory cells after each of the following sequence of statements is executed.

```
A = B / C
T = A * S
D = T + C
```

A	B	C	D	S	T
4	36	9	100 + 9 = 109	25	100 4 * 25

*5.   Suppose the following lines are executed *three* times. Show the contents of *each* memory cell after *each* execution of all three lines.

```
N = N + 1
X = X + N
S = S + X * X
```

Initially, all three cells contain zero.

After first execution.

N	X	S
1	1	1

After second execution.

N	X	S
2	3	1 + 9 = 10

After third execution.

N	X	S
3	6	10 + 36 = 46

6.   What is an application?

*7.   What is the form in the programming environment?

   8. Explain what dragging means.

   9. Describe what is meant by the user interface.

 *10. What happens to the form when a program is running?

  11. During a run, how does the user move between objects?

  12. What is a command button?

 *13. In what ways can a picture box be utilized?

  14. What control object is used to enter data?

 *15. What control object is used to identify other objects on a form?

  16. How is the caption for an object changed?

  17. What are sizing handles?

  18. What is the syntax of the Print method?

 *19. What is the purpose of the AutoSize property for a label?

  20. What type of variables can be stored in the Variant data type?

Important Terms

The following terms are introduced in this unit. Be sure you know what each of them means.

Active	Form	Properties list
Alignment property	Inactive	Properties window
Application	Interface	Property
Assignment statement	Label	Sequence structure
AutoSize property	Loop structure	Settings
BorderStyle property	Memory cell	Settings box
Caption property	Menu bar	Sizing handle
Click	Method	Structure
Cls method	Multiline property	Structured approach
Code window	Name property	Subprogram
Command button	Nonexecutable	Template
Control	Object	Text box
Control structure	Object box	Text property
Decision structure	Picture box	Title bar
Default-sized	Picture property	Toolbar
Documentation	Print method	Toolbox
Drag	Procedure	Variable
Event	Procedure box	Variable list
Event procedure	Process block	Variant
Flowchart	Project	WindowState property
Focus	Project window	

More on Interfaces and Output

2

In this unit we introduce the Format$ function and illustrate its use with a real estate application. We also explain how the Print method divides the output print line into print zones. The remaining two arithmetic operations—subtraction and exponentiation—are introduced. We close the unit with a discussion of operator hierarchy.

Learning Objectives

At the completion of this unit you should know

1. how to use the arithmetic operations subtraction and exponentiation,

2. how to use the function Format$ to format output,

3. how the Print method subdivides the print line into zones,

4. the effect of commas and semicolons in the Print method,

5. more about creating user interfaces,

6. the importance of parentheses in an arithmetic expression,

7. the importance of operator hierarchy.

Important Keyword

Format$

A Real Estate Application

After selling a house or a piece of property, a real estate broker receives a certain percentage of the selling price as a commission. The seller receives the sale price minus the broker's commission and any expenses.

To develop an application to compute the exact amount due the seller at settlement, we start with the formula

Exact Amount Due Seller = (Sale Price) × (1 - Commission) - Expenses

Next, we choose names for the variables. Let Sell stand for the exact amount due the seller, Price for the sale price, Comm for the percentage due the broker, and Expenses for the expenses. Using these names, the above formula is written in Visual Basic code as

```
Sell = Price * (1 - Comm) - Expenses
```

NOTE *The parentheses around 1 - Comm are important since Comm must be subtracted from 1 before the difference is multiplied by Price. Subtraction is denoted by the dash (-).*

Suppose that the sale price is $25,700, the broker's commission is 6%, and the seller's expenses are $119. The code for this calculation will again follow the sequence structure and can be flowchartered as shown in Figure 2.1.

As with the simple interest application, our first concern is getting the sale price, the broker's commission rate, and the expenses into the computer. To this end, we

FIGURE 2.1
A flowchart for a Real Estate application

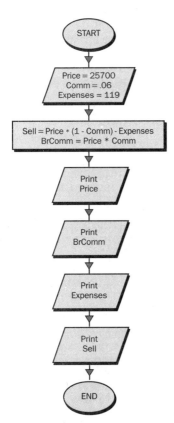

TABLE 2.1
Objects and property settings for a real estate application

OBJECT	PROPERTY	SETTING
Form	Caption	Real Estate Application
	WindowState	2-Maximized
Label1	Alignment	1-Right Justify
	Caption	Enter Sale Price
Label2	Caption	Enter Broker's Percentage Rate as a Decimal
Label3	Alignment	1-Right Justify
	Caption	Enter Expenses
Text1 box	Name	txtPrice
	Text	(blank)
Text2 box	Name	txtComm
	Text	(blank)
Text3 box	Name	txtExpenses
	Text	(blank)
Picture1 box	FontName	Courier
	Name	picRealOutput
Command1 button	Caption	Execute
	Name	cmdExecute
Command2 button	Caption	Exit
	Name	cmdExit

design a user interface using the following objects: text boxes, command buttons, labels, and a picture box for the output. We begin with a table, Table 2.1, showing the object, the properties of the object to be set, and the desired settings.

NOTE *Notice that we used the **FontName property** to set the font for the picture box. We chose the Courier font because it has a fixed pitch. This means that each character corresponds to one column in the picture window. A maximized form contains 80 columns.*

Improving the Output

So far, the output has not been expressed in a commonly used form. For instance, the interest in the simple interest application was printed with too many decimal places, that is, not to the nearest cent. This can be remedied by using the Visual Basic function Format$.

The Format$ Function—Syntax

```
Format$(expression, fmt)
```

The argument *expression* refers to the numeric value to be formatted, and the second argument *fmt* to a string of display-format characters that specify how the expression is to be printed. Format$ returns a string, that is, it converts the numeric expression into a string of characters according to the format string *fmt*. Visual Basic has several built-in format strings, or you can create your own. For our first example we'll use the built-in format called "currency." This format name instructs the computer to print the number with a dollar sign, thousand separators, where needed, and two decimal places rounded up to the nearest cent. The Format$ function converts a numerical value to a literal string of characters. For instance, Format$ (100,"currency") converts the numeric value (100) into the *string* of characters "$100.00". To show how the Format$ function works, we'll use it to print all of the variables in our current real estate application.

Here are the exact output statements we'll use:

```
picRealOutput.Print "Sale Price=", Format$(Price, "currency")
picRealOutput.Print "Broker's Commission=", Format$(BrComm, "currency")
picRealOutput.Print "Expenses=", Format$(Expenses, "currency")
picRealOutput.Print "The Exact Amount Due the Seller=", Format$(Sell, ⤶*
    "currency")
```

Adding the documentation, the complete code is shown next.

Code for the Execute Procedure

```
Rem Variable List:
Rem   BrComm = Broker's Commission
Rem   Comm = Broker's Percentage
Rem   Expenses = Expenses of the Seller
Rem   Price = Sale Price
Rem   Sell = Exact Amount Due the Seller
Rem Get the values from the text boxes
    Price = txtPrice.Text
    Comm = txtComm.Text
    Expenses = txtExpenses.Text
Rem Compute Amount Due Seller and the Broker's Commission
    Sell = Price * (1 - Comm) - Expenses
    BrComm = Price * Comm
Rem Print Data Summary and Amount Due the Seller
    picRealOutput.Cls
    picRealOutput.Print "Sale Price=", Format$(Price, "currency")
    picRealOutput.Print "Broker's Commission=", Format$(BrComm, ⤶
        "currency")
    picRealOutput.Print "Expenses=", Format$(Expenses, "currency")
    picRealOutput.Print "The Exact Amount Due the Seller=", ⤶
        Format$(Sell, "currency")
```

* The bent arrow symbol indicates that a single line of programming code has been broken across two lines in the book, only because it wouldn't print on a single line. Treat it as you would one line of code.

GUIDED ACTIVITY 2.1

Entering and Running the Real Estate Application

New features of Visual Basic contained in this activity:

- FontName property

- Format$ function

   The objective of this Guided Activity is to enter the Real Estate Application and run it.

1. Start Visual Basic.

2. Place the objects on the form in the order shown in Table 2.1. Figure 2.2 shows a suggested layout.

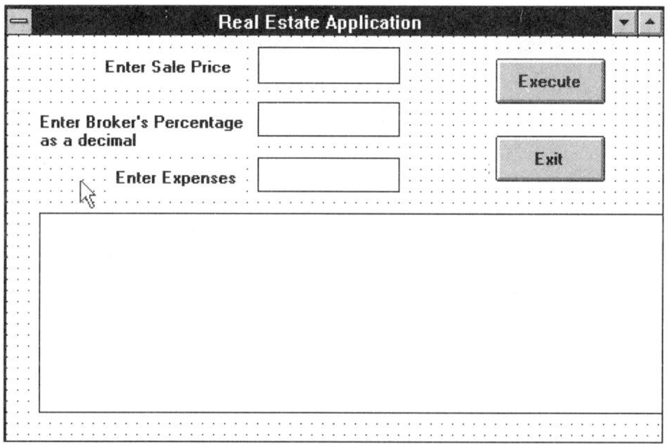

FIGURE 2.2

Interface for the Real Estate Application

3. Set the properties for each object as stated in Table 2.1.

4. Double-click the Execute button.

5. Enter the code for the event procedure cmdExecute.

6. Double-click the Exit button.

7. Enter the following lines of code.

```
Rem This procedure stops the run of the application.
End
```

8. Click the Run icon on the toolbar.

9. Enter 25700 in the first text box.

NOTE *If the cursor is not present in this box, it means that the objects were not placed on the form in the proper order. Keep pressing [Tab] until the cursor appears in the first text box or simply click the box.*

10. Press [Tab].

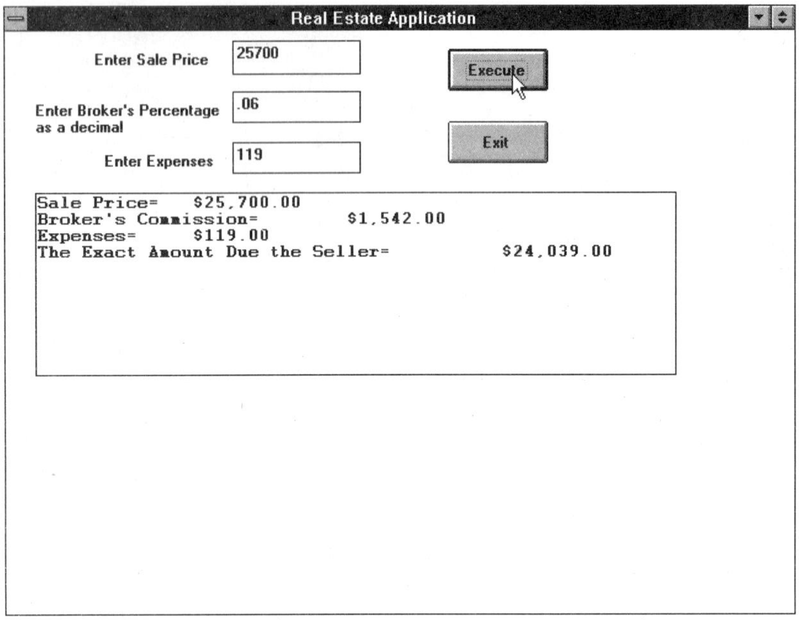

FIGURE 2.3

Result of clicking the Execute button

```
┌──────────────────────────────────────────────────────────────┐
│ ─            Real Estate Application              ▼ ▲│
├──────────────────────────────────────────────────────────────┤
│                                                                │
│    Enter Sale Price   │25700        │      ┌──────────┐        │
│                                            │ Execute  │        │
│                                            └──────────┘        │
│  Enter Broker's Percentage │.06          │                     │
│  as a decimal                                                  │
│                                            ┌──────────┐        │
│       Enter Expenses  │119          │      │   Exit   │        │
│                                            └──────────┘        │
│   ┌──────────────────────────────────────────────────────┐    │
│   │Sale Price=    $25,700.00                              │    │
│   │Broker's Commission=           $1,542.00               │    │
│   │Expenses=      $119.00                                 │    │
│   │The Exact Amount Due the Seller=        $24,039.00     │    │
│   │                                                       │    │
│   │                                                       │    │
│   │                                                       │    │
│   │                                                       │    │
│   └──────────────────────────────────────────────────────┘    │
│                                                                │
│                                                                │
│                                                                │
└──────────────────────────────────────────────────────────────┘
```

11. Enter .06 in the second box.

12. Press ⟨Tab⟩.

13. Enter 119 in the third box.

14. Press ⟨Tab⟩.

15. At this point, the Execute button should have the focus. If so, press ⟨Enter⟩. If not, click the button. Figure 2.3 shows what you should see next.

16. You may change any of the values in the three text boxes and execute the program again. For instance, click on the Broker's Percentage box.

17. Highlight the current value and type a new value, say .08.

18. Click the Execute button to obtain the new output. Try various other changes of your own choosing.

19. Save as relestap.

20. Exit Visual Basic.

    Let's examine the output of this application more closely.

NOTE *The boxed region above this output numbers the columns for reference and is not part of the output.*

```
┌────────────────────────────────────────────────────────────────────────┐
│ *    zone1    *    zone2    *    zone3    *    zone4    *    zone5       │
│ 1234567890123456789012345678901234567890123456789012345678901234567890  │
└────────────────────────────────────────────────────────────────────────┘
  Sale Price=    $25,700.00
  Broker's Commission=           $1,542.00
  Expenses=      $119.00
  The Exact Amount Due the Seller=        $24,039.00
```

Print Zones

In general, the Print method divides an output line into zones 14 spaces wide. The first position of each zone is marked with an asterisk in the boxed region. A comma between print items means "continue printing in the next zone." In the above output, the word Sale is printed in zone 1 starting with column 1. The comma between "Sale Price=" and Format$(Price, "currency") causes the computer to jump to zone 2 before printing the value of Price (25700) using the "currency" format. "Broker's Commission=" is longer than 14 characters and therefore runs into zone 2 when printed. The following comma causes a jump to zone 3 where $1,542.00 is printed. A similar explanation applies to the last two lines.

GUIDED ACTIVITY 2.2

Exploring the Print Method

New features of Visual Basic contained in this activity:

- Print zones

- TabIndex property

In this activity we explain how the Print method divides the output display into zones.

1. Start Visual Basic.

2. Place three command buttons in a row near the bottom of the form.

3. Set the properties as listed in Table 2.2.

   The table calls for the **TabIndex property** for the command buttons to be set. This is done to guarantee that pressing [Tab] during a run would cause the focus to cycle through the command buttons in the proper order.

TABLE 2.2	OBJECT	PROPERTY	SETTING
Objects and property settings for Guided Activity 2.2	Form1	Caption	Guided Activity 2.2
		FontName	Courier
		WindowState	2-Maximized
	Command1	Caption	Guide
		Name	cmdGuide
		TabIndex	0
	Command2	Caption	Run Sample
		Name	cmdSample
		TabIndex	1
	Command3	Caption	Exit
		Name	cmdExit
		TabIndex	2Text2 box

The TabIndex Property—Syntax

control.TabIndex[=*index*]

The value of *index* ranges from 0 to n-1, where n is the number of controls on the form. The tab order is assigned automatically by Visual Basic according to the order in which the controls are drawn on the form.

NOTE *If you drew the controls in the order given in the table, the TabIndex property will not need to be set.*

4. Double-click the Guide button.

5. Enter the following code for this button.

```
form1.Print "*    zone1    *    zone2    *    zone3    *    zone4    *    zone5"
form1.Print "1234567890123456789012345678901234567890123456789012345678901234567890"
```

6. Close this Code window.

CHECKPOINT 2A   How do you close a Code window?
The answers to checkpoint questions can be found in Appendix A.

7. Double-click on the Run Sample button.

8. Enter the following code for this button.

```
form1.Print "Zone 1","Zone 2","Zone 3","Zone 4","Zone 5"
```

9. Close this Code window.

10. Open the Code window for the Exit button.

11. Enter the following code.

```
End
```

12. Click the Run icon on the toolbar.

13. Click the Guide button.

14. Click the Run Sample button. The output is shown here.

```
*    zone1      *    zone2     *    zone3     *    zone4     *    zone5
12345678901234567890123456789012345678901234567890123456789001234567890
Zone 1          Zone 2          Zone 3          Zone 4          Zone 5
```

Next, we investigate what happens when the computer is told to print something containing more than 14 characters, the normal zone width.

15. Click Exit and add the following two lines to the procedure cmdSample.

```
Testval = 100
form1.Print "The Test Value is ", Testval
```

16. Run the program again by first clicking Guide followed by Run Sample. Your output should appear as shown here.

```
*   zone1      *     zone2     *     zone3     *     zone4     *     zone5
12345678901234567890123456789012345678901234567890123456789012345678901234567890

Zone 1          Zone 2          Zone 3          Zone 4          Zone 5
The Test Value is               100
```

Here we see that the value of Testval is printed in zone 3. The reason for this is that the message `The Test Value is` has 18 characters (counting the spaces), making it run into zone 2. The comma in the Print method causes the computer to jump to the next zone, zone 3, to print the value of 100.

17. Next we will see the effect of placing a comma at the end of a Print line. Add the following four lines to the code in cmdSample.

```
T = 100
S = -100
form1.Print "T equals ", T,     (Note comma here)        Comma same line
form1.Print "S equals ", S
```

18. Run the program again to see the following output.

```
*   zone1      *     zone2     *     zone3     *     zone4     *     zone5
12345678901234567890123456789012345678901234567890123456789012345678901234567890

Zone 1          Zone 2          Zone 3          Zone 4          Zone 5
The Test Value is               100
T equals        100             S equals        -100
```

In this case we see that the two new Print lines produce a single line of output. Ordinarily, each Print line encountered during a run produces a new line of output; however, a comma at the end of a line (a dangling comma) prevents the computer from advancing to a new line of output. As a result the output from the next Print line appears on the same line.

19. Remove the comma at the end of the third Print line by placing the cursor on the comma and pressing [Del]. Run again and compare the result with the output from step 18.

20. To see how you can get the computer to skip zones, add the following lines to the procedure and execute again.

```
form1.Print  "ZONE 1", ,"ZONE 3", ,"ZONE 5"
form1.Print , "ZONE 2","ZONE 3"
```

The result should be as appears here.

```
*    zone1      *     zone2      *     zone3      *     zone4      *     zone5
12345678901234567890123456789012345678901234567890123456789012345678901234567890
Zone 1          Zone 2          Zone 3          Zone 4          Zone 5
The Test Value is               100
T equals        100
S equals        -100
ZONE 1                          ZONE 3                          ZONE 5
                ZONE 2          ZONE 3
```

21. To see the effect of replacing a comma with a semicolon, edit the cmdSample procedure by replacing all of the commas with semicolons. The purpose of the semicolon is to keep the computer from advancing to the next print zone to continue printing. All spacing between print items is suppressed, as the following output shows.

22. Run the program again and study the output carefully.

```
*    zone1      *     zone2      *     zone3      *     zone4      *     zone5
12345678901234567890123456789012345678901234567890123456789012345678901234567890
Zone 1Zone 2Zone 3Zone 4Zone 5
The Test Value is  100
T equals 100
S equals -100
ZONE 1ZONE 3ZONE 5
ZONE 2ZONE 3
```

23. Exit Visual Basic without saving.

The Computer and Compound Interest

Our next application deals with compound interest. It allows the user to find the future value of an investment or the interest rate that will yield a given future value when the interest is compounded. Depending on which values are already known, the user decides what to find.

Using the Computer to Find the Future Value

Suppose we have a $10,000 investment earning interest at a rate of 11.88% compounded monthly. Let's use the computer to find the future value of this investment at the end of 30 months. The formula for the desired value is

$$S = P(1 + J / K)^N$$

where S stands for the future value, P is the present value or principal, J the annual interest rate, K the number of interest periods per year, and N the number of interest periods. The quantity J / K is known as the interest rate per interest period.

The formula calls for the quantity $(1 + J / K)$ to be raised to the power N, which is an operation known as exponentiation. It is coded in Visual Basic as

```
S = P*(1 + J / K) ^ N
```

In this formula, the circumflex ($\wedge$) (generated by [Shift][6]), is used to denote the operation exponentiation.

We take this opportunity to introduce another formatting option. The character 0 (zero) is a digit placeholder that displays a digit or a zero. If there is a digit in the value being formatted in a position corresponding to a 0 in the format string, it is displayed; otherwise a zero is displayed in that position. In the following code we'll use "0.00" as the format string for both the future value and the annual rate. The way this format works is as follows. In the case of the future value, any digits to the left of the decimal point will be displayed without modification. If there are no digits to the left of the decimal point, a zero will be displayed to the left of the decimal point. Since we have two zeros to the right of the decimal point, any value containing more than two digits will be rounded up to two places. If less than two, then trailing zeros will be displayed.

The future value is computed by the following code.

Code for the Future Value Procedure

```
Rem This procedure will calculate the future value of an investment
Rem compounded at a given rate for a given number of interest periods.
Rem Variable List:
Rem   AnnRate = Annual Interest Rate
Rem   Conv = Number of Interest Periods Per Year
Rem   FutVal = Future Value
Rem   NumIntPer = Number of Interest Periods
Rem   Princ = Principal
      AnnRate = txtAnnRate.Text
Rem Convert AnnRate to decimal
      AnnRate = AnnRate / 100
      Conv = txtConv.Text
      NumIntPer = txtNumIntPer.Text
      Princ = txtPrinc.Text
Rem Compute the Future Value
      FutVal = Princ * (1 + AnnRate / Conv) ^ NumIntPer
Rem Output result to text box txtAnnRate
      txtFutVal.Text = Format$(FutVal, "0.00")
```

Using the Computer to Find the Interest Rate

For another example of exponentiation, suppose we want to find the annual rate of interest AnnRate, given the other variables. Solving for J in our formula $S = P(1 + J / K)^N$, we obtain $J = K(S/P)^{1/N} - K$.

In terms of the code variables

```
AnnRate = Conv * (FutVal / Princ) ^ (1 / NumIntPer)-Conv
```

This formula calls for the calculation of a root—an exponentiation with a fraction for an exponent.

NOTE *Pay close attention to the placement of the parentheses in this formula. The values of* 1 / NumIntPer *and* FutVal / Princ *must each be calculated individually before the exponentiation operation can be carried out.*

Code for the Annual Rate Procedure

```
Rem This procedure finds the interest rate necessary to produce
Rem a given future value from a given principal at a given interest rate.
Rem Variable List:
Rem    AnnRate = Annual Interest Rate
Rem    Conv = Number of Interest Periods Per Year
Rem    Futval = Future Value
Rem    NumIntPer = Number of Interest Periods
Rem    Princ = Principal
       Conv = txtConv.Text
       FutVal = txtFutVal.Text
       NumIntPer = txtNumIntPer.Text
       Princ = txtPrinc.Text
Rem Compute the annual rate
       AnnRate = Conv * (FutVal / Princ) ^ (1 / NumIntPer) - Conv
Rem Output the result to text box txtAnnRate
       txtAnnRate.Text = Format$(AnnRate * 100, "0.00")
```

Figure 2.4 shows a suggested interface for our Compound Interest Application.

FIGURE 2.4
Interface for Compound Interest Application

Entering and Running the Compound Interest Application

New features of Visual Basic contained in this activity:

- FontBold property

- FontItalic property

    The purpose of this activity is to enter and run the Compound Interest Application and to demonstrate the FontBold and FontItalic properties.

1. Start Visual Basic.

2. Create the user interface as shown in Figure 2.4. Table 2.3 lists the control objects and the property settings that need to be changed.

NOTE *To draw the attention of the user to the unknowns (either the future value or the interest rate) in this application, we set the **FontBold property** and the **FontItalic property** to True for their corresponding labels.*

To further emphasize the unknowns, we set the BorderStyle to 1-Fixed Single for their labels, to cause the labels to be placed in a box.

We set the TabIndex property on all of the objects except for the labels to make sure that, regardless of the order in which they are created, tabbing will move the focus through the interface in the correct sequence.

3. Enter the code for each of the command buttons. The code for the Exit button is an End statement.

CHECKPOINT 2B What is the purpose of the third command button?

4. Click the Run icon on the toolbar.

5. Test your program by entering 12 in the first text box (when you start the run the cursor should be in this box already because you set the Tab Indexes; if not, press [Tab] until it is).

6. Press [Tab].

7. Press [Tab] again to skip the *Future Value* box (this is the variable we are solving for in this example).

8. Enter 30 in the Interest Periods box.

9. Press [Tab].

10. Enter 10000 in the Principal box.

11. Press [Tab].

12. Enter 6 in the *Annual Interest Rate* box.

13. Click on the Future Value button. You should see 11614.00 appear in the *Future Value* box on the form.

TABLE 2.3	OBJECT	PROPERTY	SETTING
Control objects and property settings	Form1	Caption	Compound Interest Application
		WindowState	2-Maximized
	Label1	Alignment	1-Right Justify
		Caption	Number of Interest Periods
	Label2	Alignment	1-Right Justify
		BorderStyle	1-Fixed Single
		Caption	Future Value
		FontBold	True
		FontItalic	True
	Label3	Alignment	1-Right Justify
		Caption	Interest Periods Per Year
	Label4	Alignment	1-Right Justify
		Caption	Principal
	Label5	Alignment	1-Right Justify
		AutoSize	True
		BorderStyle	1-Fixed Single
		Caption	Annual Interest Rate
		FontBold	True
		FontItalic	True
	Text1	Name	txtConv
		TabIndex	0
		Text	(blank)
	Text 2	Name	txtFutVal
		TabIndex	1
		Text	(blank)
	Text3	Name	txtNumIntPer
		TabIndex	2
		Text	(blank)
	Text4	Name	txtPrinc
		TabIndex	3
		Text	(blank)
	Text5	Name	txtAnnRate
		TabIndex	4
		Text	(blank)
	Command1	Caption	Future Value
		Name	cmdFutureVal
		TabIndex	5
	Command2	Caption	Annual Rate
		Name	cmdAnnRate
		TabIndex	6
	Command3	Caption	Exit
		Name	cmdExit
		TabIndex	7

14. At this point, you can change any value by highlighting the contents of any box and typing a new value. Let's try it. Highlight the contents of the Number of Interest Periods box and type 180. This changes the number of interest periods to 180.

15. Click the Future Value button. You should see 24540.94 appear in the *Future Value* box.

16. Let's solve for an interest rate. Click on the *Future Value* box and change the value to 30000. Be sure to highlight the old value so that it will be deleted when you enter 30000. There must not be any dollar sign or comma in the value entered.

17. Click and change the number of interest periods to 120.

18. Click the Annual Rate button to see what the annual rate must be for $10,000 to yield $30,000 in 10 years (120 months) compounding monthly. The answer is 11.04%.

19. Experiment on your own by changing the values of various variables and solving (remember, the program is capable of only solving for two of the five variables).

20. Save the project as cominap.

21. Exit Visual Basic.

Operator Hierarchy

Now that you have used each of the arithmetic operations, you are in a better position to understand the following, more formal discussion.

The order in which the arithmetic operations are carried out is known as the **operator hierarchy**.

Hierarchy	Operator	Operation
Highest 1.	^	Exponentiation
2.	*, /	Multiplication and division
Lowest 3.	+, −	Addition and subtraction

Having the highest priority, exponentiation is normally performed first in any expression. Next, all multiplications and divisions are performed, followed by all additions and subtractions. When the computer carries out operations on the same level, it works left to right. The above description will be considered the normal method of evaluating an expression. Parentheses are used to interrupt the normal method.

Parentheses

It was because of operator hierarchy that we emphasized the use of parentheses so much in the previous examples. Take, for instance, the formula

```
Sell = Price * (1 - Comm) - Expenses
```

used in relestap. If this formula were executed according to operator hierarchy without the parentheses, Price would be multiplied by 1, then Comm would be subtracted from that result, and, finally, Expenses would be subtracted. This would be totally wrong. An even worse calculation would result from the compound amount formula

```
S = P * (1 + J / K) ^ N
```

if the parentheses were omitted and operator hierarchy were allowed to take over. In this case, K would be raised to the power N *first* followed by P times 1 and J divided by K to the power N. S would then be evaluated as the sum of these two values. That is, $S = P + J / K^N$ according to standard notation.

In the future value formula $S = P * (1 + J / K) \wedge N$, the N stands for the number of interest periods. Occasionally, what is known is the number of years M, leaving the value of N to be calculated by multiplying M by K. In this case, the formula becomes

```
S = P * (1 + J / K) ^ (K * M)
```

The parentheses around K * M are required because operator hierarchy would cause S to be calculated incorrectly.

Expression Evaluation

To illustrate, we trace how the computer would evaluate $S = P * (1 + J / K) \wedge (K * M)$. The expressions inside the parentheses are evaluated first. Inside the first set we have 1 + J / K. Since division is on a higher level than addition, J divided by K is computed first, then 1 is added to the result. Next, the exponent K * M in the second pair of parentheses is computed. Since exponentiation has the highest priority, 1 + J / K to the power K * M is computed next. Finally, this result is multiplied by P to yield S.

Without the parentheses around K * M, the formula would be handled as $P(1 + J / K)^K M$ according to standard mathematical notation. That is, operator hierarchy would have dictated that the quantity 1 + J / K be raised to the power K first and the result multiplied by P and then by M (working left to right).

Here are some more illustrations.

- Consider how the computer would evaluate

```
A / B * C / D
```

Since the two operations are on the same level, the computer works left to right. A is divided by B first. This result is then multiplied by C, and, finally, the resulting product is divided by D. In standard mathematical notation the expression would be interpreted as follows:

```
((A / B) * C) / D
```

With A=64, B=8, C=3, and D=6, we get

```
A / B * C / D = 64 / 8 * 3 / 6
              = 8 * 3 / 6
              = 24 / 6
              = 4
```

- In the expression

  ```
  A / B + C / D
  ```

  division is one level higher than addition. Therefore, the two divisions are performed first, and the results are added. Using the same values as above, we get

  ```
  A / B + C / D = 64 / 8 + 3 / 6
                = 8 + .5
                = 8.5
  ```

- Consider the expression

  ```
  A - B * C - D
  ```

  for the values given above. First, B times C is calculated. This result is then subtracted from A and then D is subtracted. That is,

  ```
  A - B * C - D = 64 - 8 * 3 - 6
                = 64 - 24 - 6
                = 40 - 6
                = 34
  ```

- In the simple interest formula, I = PRT, we can solve for P given I, R, and T. The result is

  ```
  P = I / RT
  ```

  At first glance, we might try to code this as

  ```
  P = I / R * T
  ```

  However, according to operator hierarchy, this would actually be treated as

  ```
  P = (I / R) * T
  ```

  which is equivalent to

  ```
  P = IT / R
  ```

  in standard mathematical notation. Hence, it must be coded as

  ```
  P = I / (R * T)
  ```

  The parentheses force the computer to multiply R by T before dividing into I. This formula could also be coded as

  ```
  P = I / R / T
  ```

  since the computer will divide I by R first and then divide this result by T, which, mathematically speaking, is the same as dividing I by the product of R and T.

- For our final illustration, consider the formula

  ```
  A / B ^ C * D
  ```

In this case, the exponentiation would be carried out first. Then, the result would be divided into A and that result multiplied by D. Here is how it goes with the above numbers.

```
A / B ^ C * D = 64 / 8 ^ 3 * 6
= 64 / 512 * 6
= 0.125 * 6
= .75
```

Keyword Syntax Review

Keyword—Syntax	Purpose
Format$(*expression, fmt*)	To specify how an expression should be formatted

EXERCISE 2.1

Sale Price for a Home

Using relestap as a model, build an application (interface and procedures) to find the sale price, given the exact amount due the seller, the broker's percentage, and the expenses. Use the formula

```
Price = (Sell + Expenses) / (1 - Comm)
```

The parentheses in this formula are important and cannot be omitted. Test the program using Sell = 25,500, Expenses = 119, and Comm = 6%. The output should be Price = $27,254.26.

EXERCISE 2.2

Compound Interest Rate

Using cominap as a model and the formula for the principal

```
Princ = FutVal * (1 + J / Conv) ^ (-NumIntPer)
```

build an application to find the principal required to reach a given future value. Test your program using Conv = 12, FutVal = 3500, J = 11.24%, and NumIntPer = 60. The output should be Princ = 2000.

EXERCISE 2.3

Property Value

The value of a property is given by the following formula:

Value = (Net Income) / (Rate Demanded by Capital)

The formula for *Rate Demanded by Capital* is

*Rate = Yield Rate - (Mortgage Ratio)(Mortgage Coefficient) +
    (Depreciation)(Sinking Fund Factor)*

Create an application to find *Value* given the *Net Income,* the *Yield Rate,* the *Mortgage Ratio,* the *Mortgage Coefficient,* the *Depreciation,* and the *Sinking Fund Factor.* Test your program using a *Net Income* of 5000, a *Yield Rate* of .07, a *Mortgage Ratio* of .67, a *Mortgage Coefficient* of .0134, a *Depreciation* of .25, and a *Sinking Fund Factor* of .0724. The output should be a *Value* of $63,193.55.

EXERCISE 2.4

Mortgage Coefficient

The formula for a mortgage coefficient C is

```
C = Y + P / S - F
```

where Y is the yield rate, P is the percentage of the mortgage to be amortized, S is the annuity factor, and F is the annual requirement. Create an application to find C, then test it using Y = .07, P = .67, S = 13.812, and F = .098063. The output should be C = .02044.

EXERCISE 2.5

Stopping Distance

The formula to calculate the stopping distance D of a moving automobile is

```
D = V * 2.25 + V ^ 2 / 21
```

where V is the speed of the car in miles per hour. Create an application to find D given V. Test the program for several choices for V. The stopping distance at 25 mph is 86 feet.

EXERCISE 2.6

Discount

When a store decides to discount an item by a certain percentage, the sale price is computed by subtracting the discount from the original or base price. Thus, the sale price S = B - D where B is the base price and D is the discount. If R is the percentage of discount, then D = B * R / 100. Create an application to find the discount and the sale price of an item given the base price and the percentage of discount. Test the program for an item with a base price of $499.95 and a discount rate of 19%. The output should be a discount of $94.99 and a sale price of $404.96.

EXERCISE 2.7

Loan Payment Analysis

Each loan payment is divided into two parts—interest and principal payment. The principal payment is subtracted from the current balance. The interest is $\frac{1}{12}$ the annual interest rate in decimal times the current balance.

*Interest = Balance * Rate / 12*

The principal payment is the payment less the interest.

Principal = Payment - Interest

The new balance is the old balance less the principal payment.

Balance = Balance - Principal

Create an application that will output the interest, the principal payment, and the new balance in a picture box given the current balance, the interest rate, and the payment. To test your application, let current balance = 10000000, payment = 195662.90, and rate = .065. Then the interest payment should be $54,166.67, the principal payment should be $141,496.20, and the new balance should be $9,858,504.00.

EXERCISE 2.8

Temperature Conversion

The formula to convert a Fahrenheit temperature F to its corresponding Celsius temperature C is C = (5 / 9)(F - 32), and the formula to convert a Celsius temperature to Fahrenheit is F = (9 / 5) * C +32. Create an application to convert a Fahrenheit temperature entered into a text box to its Celsius equivalent displayed in another text box and vice versa. Use two command buttons to make it possible for the user to choose which type of conversion he or she desires. The output for 72 degrees Fahrenheit should be 22.2222 degrees Celsius, while 100 degrees Celsius is equivalent to 212 degrees Fahrenheit.

Review Questions

The answers to questions marked with an asterisk are contained in Appendix A.

1. If A = 3 and B = 6, what is the value of C = A * B * (B / A - 1)? What is the value of C = A * B * (B / (A - 1))?

*2. If A = 2 and B = 5, find Y = A + 25 * A / 5 ^ A / B / 4. Show how you arrived at your answer.

3. What is the syntax for the Format$ function?

*4. How long is a Print zone?

5. What is the effect of a comma between print items in a print statement?

*6. How do you keep the Print method from advancing to a new line to continue printing?

7. What is the effect of the format string "currency" on a numeric value?

8. What symbol denotes exponentiation?

*9. What format string converts numeric output to a percentage?

*10. Let A = 695.568. What does Format$(A,"currency") equal?

11. Let A = 11.2567. What does Format$(A,"percent") equal?

*12. How do you output a value of the variable Taxes in dollars and cents format to a text box named txtTax?

13. How would you output the value of a variable called Account through a text box named txtBalance?

14. Let a picture box have the name picOutput. Write a statement that would print `The Balance is $100.00` in the picture box.

15. Explain why parentheses are useful when writing arithmetic expressions.

16. What is the function of the TabIndex property?

17. What is the result of setting the FontItalic property to True for a label?

18. How would you get the output to be in bold print in a picture box?

19. How can you change the font for a text box?

Important Terms

FontBold property	FontName property	TabIndex property
FontItalic property	Operator hierarchy	

Loop Structures

This unit introduces the second fundamental logic structure, called the loop structure. This structure is used whenever we want to execute a sequence of statements repeatedly. Two types of looping statements are discussed and illustrated.

Learning Objectives

At the completion of this unit you should know

1. the pre-test and post-test loop structure,

2. how to construct a Do Until loop and a Do While loop,

3. how to construct a For/Next loop,

4. how to use relational expressions,

5. how to calculate a sum of numbers.

Important Keywords

Do

For

InputBox

Loop

Next

Or

Screen

SetFocus

Spc

Tab

Until

While

Introduction to Loops

Consider the problem of repeatedly executing the steps shown in Figure 3.1.

The process of repeating a sequence of steps is known as *looping*. This brings us to the *second* fundamental logic structure, called the *loop structure*, mentioned in Unit 1.

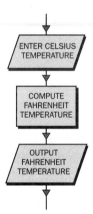

FIGURE 3.1
Flowchart for converting Celsius to Fahrenheit

ENTER CELSIUS TEMPERATURE

COMPUTE FAHRENHEIT TEMPERATURE

OUTPUT FAHRENHEIT TEMPERATURE

Loop Structure

A *loop* is formed by a block of Visual Basic statements that are to be executed repeatedly. Every loop has two main components. The first is the block of statements to be executed, called the *body of the loop*, and the second consists of the *loop control statements*. The loop control statements determine how many times the body of the loop will be executed or the condition under which the loop will be terminated.

Pre-Test Structure and Post-Test Structure

A loop is formed in one of two ways, by using either a *pre-test structure* or a *post-test structure*. In the pre-test structure, the body of the loop *follows* the test for termination, whereas in the post-test structure the body of the loop *precedes* the test. An important difference is that the post-test loop is always executed *at least once*. Figure 3.2 shows flowcharts for each type.

FIGURE 3.2
*Flowcharts for
the two types of
loop structures*

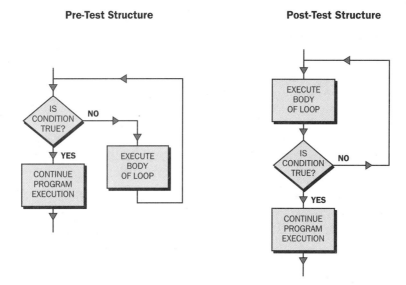

To implement a loop structure we use either the Do Until/Loop, the Do While/Loop, or the Do/Until Loop statement combination.

The Pretest Do Until/Loop Combination

Let's continue with our program to convert Celsius temperatures to Fahrenheit temperatures. We want the computer to keep asking for a temperature to convert until the user decides to stop. Letting Celsius stand for the Celsius temperature and Fahren for the Fahrenheit temperature, the conversion formula is Fahren = (9 / 5) * Celsius + 32. The value of Celsius to be converted will be entered by means of the **InputBox function**. We'll use the value obtained for this function as the **loop control variable**, and we'll use a null string as the condition to terminate the loop.

The InputBox Function—Syntax

InputBox(*prompt* [,[*title*][,[*default*][, *xpos,ypos*]]])

The *prompt* is a message that is displayed in the dialog box generated by the function. The message must be no more than 255 characters. The optional *title* is a caption displayed on the title bar of the dialog box. The *default* is the value returned by the function if the user fails to enter a value. It is displayed in a text box within the dialog box. If omitted, the text box is empty and the function returns an empty string (""). *Xpos* and *ypos* determine the horizontal distance and the vertical distance of the left edge and the upper edge, respectively, of the dialog box from the left edge of the screen. If omitted, the dialog box is centered horizontally and vertically placed about one-third of the way down the screen. If you use *xpos* and *ypos* without using either *title*, or *default*, or both, then you must use the commas between the function arguments. The value returned to the program by the InputBox function is a Variant data

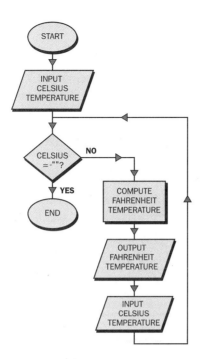

FIGURE 3.3
A flowchart for a temperature conversion program with a loop

type. By default, the type is a string. Remember, Visual Basic automatically converts a string value to a numeric form if used in an arithmetic expression. We take advantage of this in what follows.

Next, we draw a flowchart shown in Figure 3.3.

The flowchart calls for a pre-test loop. The pre-test Do Until loop using the Do Until/Loop statement combination uses the following general format.

Pre-test Do Until/Loop Combination—Syntax

```
Do Until condition under which the loop terminates
    [ body of the loop ]
Loop
```

For our current application, the *loop control statement*s are

```
Do Until Celsius = ""
```

and

```
Loop
```

For the *body of the loop* we use

```
Fahren = (9 / 5) * Celsius + 32
txtFahren.Text = Fahren
Celsius = InputBox(Msg, Title, , 0, 0)
```

The Do Until loop gets its name from the fact that the loop statements are executed *until* the controlling condition is true. The Loop statement serves two functions:

- It marks the physical end of the loop.

- It causes the computer to branch back to the Do Until statement to check if the loop should be executed again.

The Do Until/Loop combination is just one of several looping techniques available in Visual Basic.

The user interface is shown in Figure 3.4.

The settings for the objects shown in the user interface are listed in Table 3.1.

Code for the Enter Celsius Command Button

```
Sub Command1_Click ()
      Msg = "Please enter a Celsius temperature. To stop click Cancel"
      Title = "Enter Celsius Temperature"
      Celsius = InputBox(Msg, Title, , 0, 0)
      Do Until Celsius = ""
          Fahren = (9 / 5) * Celsius + 32
          txtFahren.Text = Fahren
          Celsius = InputBox(Msg, Title, , 0, 0)
      Loop
End Sub
```

TABLE 3.1

*Objects and
property
settings for
Celsius to
Fahrenheit
converter
application*

OBJECT	PROPERTY	SETTING
Form	Caption	Celsius to Fahrenheit Converter
	WindowState	2-Maximized
Command1	Caption	Enter Celsius
	TabIndex	0
Command2	Caption	Exit
	TabIndex	1
Text1 box	Name	txtFahren
	TabIndex	2
Label1	Caption	The Fahrenheit Temperature is

Let's trace through the loop. As long as Celsius is *not* equal to "", the lines of the body of the loop will be executed. The Loop statement causes the computer to branch back to the Do Until statement. At this point the Do Until statement tests the value of Celsius entered by the user via the InputBox function. If Celsius = "", then control of the program is passed to the first line after the Loop statement. In this case that would be End Sub.

To make sure we thoroughly understand this loop, suppose we delete the call to the InputBox function just before the Loop statement. This would create an *endless* or *infinite loop*. Do you see why? Consider what happens at the start of the run. Assume that a value not equal to "" is entered for Celsius. Since Celsius is not "", the loop statements are executed and the Loop statement returns control to the Do Until statement. What happens? Well, the value of Celsius is the same and therefore the loop is executed again with the same value for Celsius! Thus, we have a "runaway" or endless loop since there is no way to stop it except by interrupting the run using Ctrl Break . Consequently, we must give the user an opportunity to enter the next Celsius temperature to be converted *within* the loop.

Running the Celsius to Fahrenheit Converter

New feature of Visual Basic contained in this activity:

- InputBox function

The purpose of this activity is to run the Celsius to Fahrenheit Converter so that you can see how the Input Box function works in an actual run.

1. Start Visual Basic.

2. Create the user interface as shown in Figure 3.4.

3. Enter the code for the Enter Celsius command button.

4. Click the Run icon on the toolbar and click the Enter Celsius button. Figure 3.5 shows what you will see next. In the upper-left corner of the screen is the dialog box generated by the InputBox function. The cursor should be blinking in the text box in this box.

5. Enter 100 and click OK. The corresponding Fahrenheit temperature of 212 should appear in the text box on the form.

6. Try entering another Celsius temperature and click OK.

7. When you are tired of converting temperatures, click Cancel. This closes the dialog box.

8. Click the Exit button.

9. Double-click the Enter Celsius button.

FIGURE 3.5
*User interface
at run time*

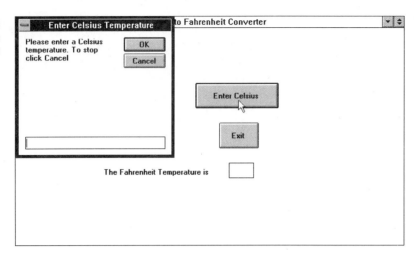

10. Change the call to the InputBox function just before the Loop statement to a remark by placing an apostrophe at the beginning of the line. Recall that an apostrophe can be used in place of Rem.

11. Click the Run icon on the toolbar again.

12. Click the Enter Celsius button.

13. Enter 100 for the Celsius temperature.

14. Click OK. What happens next? Notice that the computer seems to be "locked up," that is, the mouse has no effect. The keyboard seems dead. Why? The computer is caught in an infinite loop. Actually, it is continually printing 212 in the text box, but the human eye cannot detect this action.

15. Press Ctrl Break to interrupt the run.

16. Double-click the Enter Celsius command button and delete the apostrophe you entered in step 10.

17. Save the application as celfah.

18. Exit Visual Basic.

Relational Expressions or Boolean Expressions

The *"condition under which the loop terminates"* is a **relational expression** that can assume one of two **truth values**—"true" or "false." For example, the condition (Celsius = "") in the program celfah is a relational expression that has a truth value of "true" when Celsius = "" (an empty string) and the value "false" when it does not. In general, any expression that has a truth value of true or false is called a **Boolean expression** (after George Boole, an English mathematician and logician). All relational expressions are examples of Boolean expressions.

Relational expressions are formed using the six **relational operators** shown in Table 3.2.

TABLE 3.2	SYMBOL	MEANING	EXAMPLE
Relational operators	<	is less than	AGE + T < 25 * YRS
	>	is greater than	TIME > 1100
	=	is equal to	A = 34
	<>	is not equal to	RATE <> .06
	<=	is less than or is equal to	EMPL <= 6
	>=	is greater than or is equal to	NET >= 15

NOTE *The literal meaning of "<>" is "less than or greater than." It translates into "not equal to" because if a number is less than or greater than another, they must not be equal. Notice that calculations are permitted in relational expressions.*

The Pretest Do While/Loop Combination

The loop in celfah could be constructed using the Do While/Loop combination, with a few minor changes. First, we would replace `Until` with `While`. Second, we would need to change the condition under which the loop terminates. In this case, the loop statements are to be executed *While* the condition is true, not *Until* it is true. The loop is terminated when the truth value of the condition is *false*. Hence, we use Celsius <> "". The new control line would be

```
Do While Celsius <> ""
```

Everything else in the program stays the same.

A flowchart for a Do While loop is shown in Figure 3.6

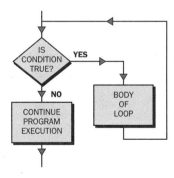

FIGURE 3.6
A flowchart for a pre-test Do While loop

NOTE *The placement of the words NO and YES in Figure 3.6 do not agree with the pre-test structure in Figure 3.2 since it is a Do While loop that is executed as long as the condition is true.*

There is virtually no difference between a Do Until loop and a Do While loop. The former loop is executed *until* a relational expression becomes true and the latter *while* it is true. Since the end result is the same, any Do Until loop can be written as a Do While loop and vice versa.

Pre-Test Do While/Loop Combination—Syntax

```
Do While condition under which the loop terminates
      [ body of the loop ]
Loop
```

The Post-Test Do/Loop Until Combination

In the *post-test* form of the Do Until loop, the controlling condition is tested *after* the loop is executed. The loop statements must be executed at least once to reach the condition and determine its truth value. This guarantees that the loop will be executed at least once. For example, consider an ATM (automated teller machine) transaction at your bank. The customer must enter a PIN (personal identification number) before the transaction can be completed. The loop that asks for the number must be executed at least once and will not continue if the wrong PIN number is entered. Here is a program segment that could be used to handle this situation.

```
PIN = "1234"
Msg = "Please enter your PIN and click OK"
Do
      Pass = InputBox(Msg)
Loop Until Pass = PIN Or Pass = ""
```

The procedure begins by assigning the correct PIN to the variable called PIN. When the value assigned is a string of characters in quotes and the default data type is Variant, PIN automatically becomes a *string variable*. A value for a string variable is simply a string of characters enclosed by quotation marks. The InputBox returns a string through the variable Pass that would presumably be the correct PIN. However, the user may choose to cancel by clicking the Cancel button in the dialog box issued by InputBox. In that case, Pass is an empty string (""). The possibility of two choices leads us to introduce the *logical operator* Or so that the loop will terminate when the *compound condition*, Pass = PIN Or Pass = "", is true. A compound condition using Or is true if, and only if, *at least* one of the component conditions is true. Table 3.3, called a *truth table*, shows the truth value for Condition 1 Or Condition 2 for all possible truth values of the conditions.

	CONDITION 1	CONDITION 2	CONDITION 1 OR CONDITION 2
TABLE 3.3 *Truth table for the logical operator Or*	true	true	true
	true	false	true
	false	true	true
	false	false	false

Thus, the correct PIN value Or a click on Cancel will terminate the loop. There are two other logical operators, called And and Not. They will be introduced later on in the text.

It should be clear that for this loop structure to work correctly, the loop control variable must be changed somewhere in the body of the loop. Otherwise, an infinite loop will result.

The syntax of a post-test Do Until loop using the Do/Loop Until statement combination is given next.

Post-Test Do/Loop Until Combination—Syntax

```
Do
    [ body of the loop ]
Loop Until condition under which the loop terminates
```

GUIDED ACTIVITY 3.2

Executing the ATM Example

This activity demonstrates the post-test loop structure.

1. Start Visual Basic.

2. Draw two command buttons on the form.

3. Change the caption to Enter PIN on the first button.

4. Change the caption on the other to Exit.

5. Open the Code window for the Exit command

CHECKPOINT 3A How do you open a Code window for a command button?

6. Enter the End statement into the procedure.

7. Switch to the Code window for the Enter PIN command button.

CHECKPOINT 3B How do you switch between Code windows?

8. Enter the code as given in the text.

9. Click the Run icon on the toolbar.

10. Click the Enter PIN button and enter 2413 as the PIN.

11. Click OK.

12. Now, enter the correct PIN, which is 1234.

13. Click Enter PIN button.

14. Click Cancel in the dialog box issued by the InputBox function.

15. Save as atm.

CHECKPOINT 3C Which icon do you click to save a project?

16. Exit Visual Basic.

Trial-and-Error Using a Post-Test Do/Loop Until Loop

To further illustrate this type of loop structure, suppose we want to know how many interest periods it will take for an investment of, say, $10,000 to at least double in value at a given compound interest rate. To solve this problem, we will write an application to calculate successive future values of any principal entered by the user until it equals or exceeds twice as much.

The future value formula is

```
S = P * (1+J/K) ^ N
```

where P = the principal, J = the annual interest rate, K = the frequency of interest periods per year, and N = the number of interest periods. To find the proper N, we use a trial-and-error method where the computer continues to calculate S until it exceeds or equals twice the original principal P. The post-test loop structure is well suited to this task since we need to find S for at least one period and perhaps more.

We begin with the user interface shown in Figure 3.7.

FIGURE 3.7
User interface for Doubling Time Application

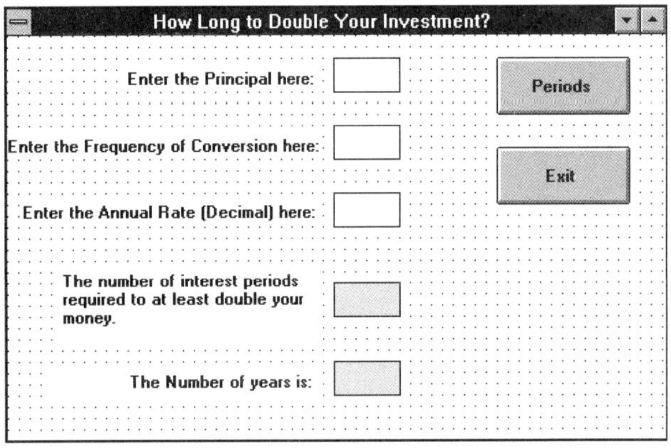

Table 3.4 lists the property settings for the objects on the interface.

TABLE 3.4	OBJECT	PROPERTY	SETTING
Property settings for the Doubling Time Application	Command1	Caption	Periods
		Name	cmdNumPrds
		TabIndex	3
	Command2	Caption	Exit
		Name	cmdExit
		TabIndex	4
	Label1	Alignment	1-Right Justify
		AutoSize	True
		Caption	Enter the Principal here:
		TabIndex	5

OBJECT	PROPERTY	SETTING
Label2	Alignment	1-Right Justify
	AutoSize	True
	Caption	Enter the Frequency of Conversion here:
	TabIndex	6
Label3	Alignment	1-Right Justify
	AutoSize	True
	Caption	Enter the Annual Rate (Decimal) here:
	TabIndex	7
Label4	Caption	The number of interest periods required to at least double your money
	TabIndex	8
Label5	Alignment	1-Right Justify
Text1	Name	txtPrincipal
	TabIndex	0
	Text	(blank)
Text2	Name	txtFrequency
	TabIndex	1
	Text	(blank)
Text3	Name	txtAnnRate
	TabIndex	2
	Text	(Blank)
Text4	BackColor	Yellow
	Name	txtNumPrds
	TabIndex	10
Text5	BackColor	Yellow
	Name	txtNumYrs
	TabIndex	11

Next, we draw a flowchart shown in Figure 3.8.
Following the flowchart, we code the loop as

```
Do
     N = N+1
Rem Compute the future value for the next period
     S = P * (1 + J /K ) ^ N
Loop Until S >= 2 * P
```

The value of N is initialized outside the loop at zero. The first line of the loop body makes N = 1 and then the future value for one period is calculated. If the value equals or exceeds twice the original principal, then the loop is terminated and the value of N is output. Otherwise, N is incremented and the future value is calculated

FIGURE 3.8

A flowchart for a procedure to find the number of periods required to at least double a given principal

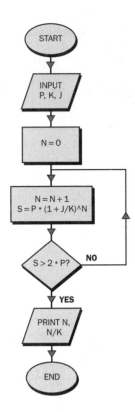

again. This process will continue until S is greater than or equal to twice the principal P.

Here is the entire code for the procedure.

Procedure for the Doubling Time Application

```
'       Variable list:
'       J = Annual Interest Rate (Decimal)
'       K = Number of Interest Periods per Year
'       N = Number of Interest Periods
'       P = Principal
'       S = Future Value
Rem   Get Variables
      P = txtPrincipal.Text
      K = txtFrequency.Text
      J = txtAnnRate.Text
Rem   Initialize Variable N
      N = 0
Rem   Change Mouse Pointer to an Hourglass
      Screen.MousePointer = 11
Do
      N = N+1
Rem   Compute the future value for the next period
      S = P * (1 + J /K ) ^ N
```

```
Loop Until S >= 2 * P
Rem   Change the Mouse Pointer to default type
      Screen.MousePointer = 0
Rem   Output the required number of periods and years
      txtNumPrds.Text = N
      txtNumYrs.Text = N / K
```

When the user clicks the Periods button, it may appear, at first, that nothing is happening. To let the user know that some computation is taking place and to wait for the calculating to finish, we use the **MousePointer property** to change the pointer to an hourglass until the loop is complete. It is then restored to normal. The necessary lines of code are

```
Screen.MousePointer = 11
```

and

```
Screen.MousePointer = 0
```

The lead word Screen refers to the **Screen object** and means that the pointer changes across the *entire* screen. The setting 11 refers to the hourglass, the standard Windows symbol that means to wait. The setting 0 refers to the default setting (the usual Windows setting), which causes the shape of the pointer to be determined by the control it happens to be over. There are 13 settings from which to choose. Consult the *Language Reference* for more information.

MousePointer Property—Syntax

```
Screen.MousePointer [=setting]
```

or

```
[form.][control.] MousePointer [=setting]
```

GUIDED ACTIVITY 3.3

Running the Doubling Time Application

New features of Visual Basic contained in this activity:

- BackColor property
- More on formatting
- MousePointer property
- Screen object

This activity demonstrates three new properties and further illustrates the post-test loop structure.

1. Start Visual Basic.

2. Create the interface shown in Figure 3.7 using the settings given in Table 3.4.

3. Enter the doubling time procedure code in the Code window for the Periods button.

4. Enter an End statement as the code for the Exit command.

5. Run the application and enter 1000 for P, 12 for K, and .08 for J. The number of periods should be 105 and the number of years 8.75.

6. Change the interest rate to .06.

CHECKPOINT 3D How do you change a value in a text box?

7. Click the Periods button. The output this time is 139 periods and 11.583 years.

8. Click the Stop run icon on the toolbar.

9. Change the last line (txtNumYrs.Text = N / K) to `txtNumYrs.Text = Format$(N / K, "#")`.

10. Try a run using the same data as in step 5. Note how the new format string rounds the number of years up to the nearest whole number of years. The format character # is called a *digit placeholder*. If there is a digit in the value of N / K in the position where # appears, it is printed. If the value N / K has a fractional part, the Format$ function rounds up to the nearest whole number. For more information on the # format character, consult the *Language Reference*.

11. Change the Principal to 2500 and click the Periods button. What do you notice?

12. Change the Principal to 15000 and click the Periods button. What do you notice this time? Steps 10, 11, and 12 should make you realize that the amount of the Principal does not matter. The doubling time is still the same. Can you explain why?

13. Save as `numprds`.

14. Exit Visual Basic.

About the New Feature in Guided Activity 3.3

The *BackColor property* sets the background color of an object. You can choose the color you want by selecting a color from the Properties window. A selection of choices is displayed by clicking the arrow box on the Settings box.

For/Next Loops

The For/Next statement combination provides another method for creating a pre-test loop using a *counter*. The counter is the loop control variable. The For statement marks the beginning of the loop and the Next the end. The body of the loop lies between these two statements. Figure 3.9 shows a flowchart for a For/Next loop.

FIGURE 3.9
A flowchart for a For/Next loop

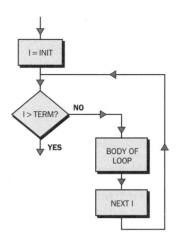

For/Next Loop—Syntax

For *control variable = initial value* To *terminal value* [Step *increment*]
    [*body of the loop*]
Next *control variable*

As an example, we'll write an application to create a table of equivalent Celsius and Fahrenheit temperatures. Recall the formula for converting a Celsius temperature into Fahrenheit:

```
Fahren = (9 / 5) * Celsius + 32
```

Let's begin by planning the user interface. We'll allow the user to choose the beginning Celsius temperature, but to make sure the table does not get too large for the screen, we'll choose the terminal value and the step value. Figure 3.10 shows the user interface.

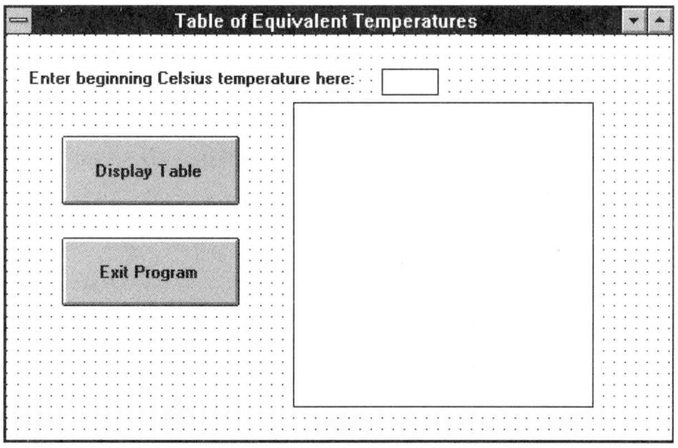

FIGURE 3.10
User interface for an equivalent temperature table

Table of Equivalent Temperatures

Enter beginning Celsius temperature here:

Display Table

Exit Program

Here is the code for the Display Table button.

Procedure for Display Table Command Button

```
Sub cmdTable_Click ()
'     Variable List:
'         Celsius = Celsius temperature
'         Fahren = Fahrenheit temperature
' Clear the picture box and print table headings
      picOutput.Cls
      picOutput.Print "Celsius", "Fahrenheit"
' Set loop limits
      Initial = txtCelsius: Terminal = Initial + 100
      For Celsius = Initial To Terminal Step 10
          Fahren = (9 / 5) * Celsius + 32
          picOutput.Print Tab(2); Celsius; Tab(18); Fahren
      Next Celsius
' Prepare Celsius text box for another beginning temperature
      txtCelsius.Text = ""
      txtCelsius.SetFocus
End Sub
```

Let's take a closer look at what's new in this procedure (see the boldfaced lines). First, note that the two lines setting up the loop limits are entered as one line separated by a colon. You may place more than one statement of code on the same line, as long as the statements are separated by a colon. Next, consider the picOutput.Print line within the loop. The new feature here is the *Tab function*. Like the tab on a typewriter, the function Tab(*column*) can be used to print output in any column of an output line. The value of the *argument*, *column*, determines where the first character of the output is printed. In the current example, the Celsius temperature is printed starting in column 2 and the Fahrenheit temperature starts in column 18. When using Tab, print items must be separated by semicolons. For more information on the Tab function, consult the *Language Reference*.

NOTE *You may have to experiment with the value of the argument due to the inexactness of the size of the picture box. After examining a trial run, you may need to resize the picture box or adjust your tabs.*

The last new items are contained in the final two statements of the procedure. The statement txtCelsius.Text = " " clears the Celsius text box by changing the contents to an empty string. The last statement, txtCelsius.SetFocus, activates the *SetFocus method*, which sets the focus to this text box. What the user sees is a blinking cursor in an empty text box. This makes it easier for the user to enter another Celsius temperature. Otherwise, the user would need to click the text box, delete its contents, and enter a new value. Of course, the user must still click the Exit Program button to stop the run.

The For Statement—Syntax

$$\text{For} \begin{Bmatrix} control \\ variable \end{Bmatrix} = \begin{Bmatrix} initial \\ value\ of \\ control \\ variable \end{Bmatrix} \text{To} \begin{Bmatrix} terminal \\ value\ of \\ control \\ variable \end{Bmatrix} \text{Step} \begin{Bmatrix} incremental \\ value\ of \\ control \\ variable \end{Bmatrix}$$

The control variable may be any valid numeric variable name. It controls the number of times the loop statements are executed. The initial value, the terminal value, and the incremental value of the control variable may all be numeric variable names or arithmetic expressions. The step part of this statement may be omitted and, when it is, Visual Basic assumes that the step is 1.

When a For statement with a *positive* step value is executed for the first time, the following activities are carried out by the computer.

1. The initial value, the terminal value, and the incremental value (if present) expressions are evaluated.

2. The initial value is assigned to the loop control variable.

3. The value of the loop control variable is compared to the terminal value.

4. If the loop control variable is less than or equal to the terminal value, then the loop statements are executed.

5. If the loop control variable is greater than the terminal value, then the loop statements are not executed. The execution of the program continues with the first statement following the Next statement.

Each time a For is encountered, after the first, it repeats steps 3, 4, and 5. Eventually, the control variable exceeds the terminal value (unless there is a program error or the step value is negative), and the loop is terminated as described in step 5.

The Next Statement—Syntax

Next *loop control variable name*

The Next statement terminates the loop. The loop control variable named in the Next statement must agree with the control variable named in the corresponding For statement. The statements between the For statement and the Next statement form the body of the loop.

If the step value is *positive*, then each time a Next statement is encountered the following activities are carried out by the computer.

1. The step value given in the corresponding For statement is added to the loop control variable. If no step value was given, +1 is added.

2. The new value of the loop control variable is compared to the terminal value.

3. If the new value of the loop control variable is less than or equal to the terminal value, the loop statements are executed again.

4. If the new value is greater than the terminal value, the loop is terminated and the run continues with the statement following the corresponding Next statement.

If the incremental value is *negative*, the Next statement *decreases* the value of the control variable. Therefore, the loop body is executed as long as the control variable is *greater than* or *equal to* the terminal value and the loop is exited when it is *less than* the terminal value.

NOTE *The step value must never be zero. If it is, an endless loop will result.*

Examples

1. `For Count = Start To Finish Step Delta`

   This is a valid For statement, provided that Start, Finish, and Delta have been assigned values before execution. Delta is either a positive or negative integer. If Delta=1, the Step Delta may be omitted.

2. `For I = 1 To 50 Step 2`

   The step value 2 causes the Next statement to increment the control variable by 2. Hence, I equals 1, 3, 5, and so on.

3. `For Count = 50 To -4 Step -2`

   The step value -2 causes the Next statement to *subtract* 2 (add minus 2) from the control variable. In this case, Count equals 50, 48, 46, and so on until it reaches -6, which would cause the loop to terminate.

4. `For Index = N ^ 2 To M + K Step 2 * N`

   In this example, N, M, and K must all have a value when this line is encountered. When it is first encountered, the initial value, the terminal value, and the incremental value must be calculated since they are arithmetic expressions. The For statement does these calculations.

GUIDED ACTIVITY 3.4

Using For/Next Loops and Summation

New features of Visual Basic contained in this activity:

- Multiple statement lines
- SetFocus method
- Summing numbers
- Tab function

   The objective is to demonstrate a For/Next loop and to introduce summations.

1. Start Visual Basic.

2. Draw the interface shown in Figure 3.10.

3. Set the Caption property for the form to `Table of Equivalent Tempera-tures`.

4. Set the other captions according to Figure 3.10.

5. Name the Display Table button `cmdTable`.

6. Name the Exit Program button `cmdExit` and enter an End statement into its Code window.

7. Name the Text box `txtCelsius`.

8. Name the Picture box `picOutput`.

9. Switch to the Display Table button using the Object box in the Code window and enter the procedure code given above.

10. Run the application and enter `0` for the beginning Celsius temperature.

11. If necessary, stop the run and resize the picture box, and then restart the run.

12. Enter `100` as the beginning Celsius temperature.

13. Enter `-40` as the beginning temperature. Do you notice anything interesting in the table?

14. Stop the run.

15. Save the project as `tmptbl`.

16. Start a new project.

CHECKPOINT 3E How do you start a new project?

17. Create the interface shown in Figure 3.11. The two boxes shown are text boxes. Be sure to make them large enough.

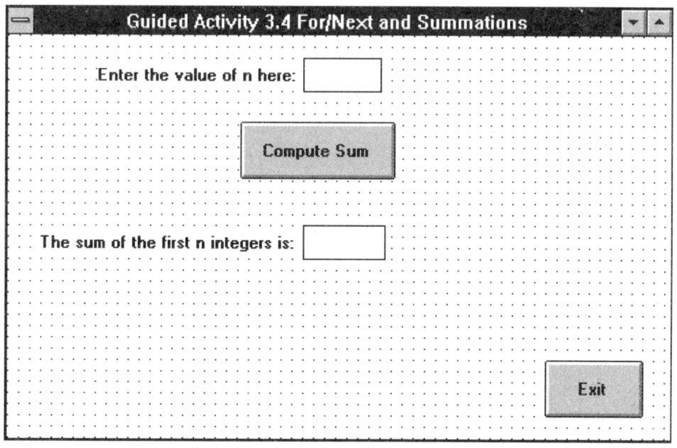

FIGURE 3.11
User interface for Guided Activity 3.4

18. Name the top text box `txtnValue` and the bottom one `txtSum`.

19. Name the Compute Sum button `cmdTable`.

20. Enter the following code for the object cmdTable.

```
Sub cmdTable_Click ()
n = txtnValue.Text
Accum = 0
For i = 1 To n
     Accum = Accum + i
Next i
txtSum.Text = Accum
txtnValue.Text = ""
txtnValue.SetFocus
End Sub
```

21. Click the Run icon.

22. Enter 3 in the n value box and click the Compute Sum button. A sum of 6 should appear in the sum box. Check: 1 + 2 + 3 = 6.

23. Enter 4 and click the Compute Sum button. Output is 10. Check: 1 + 2 + 3 + 4 = 10.

24. Enter 5 and click the Compute Sum button. Output is 15. Check: 1 + 2 + 3 + 4 + 5 = 15.

25. Click Exit.

From the output of steps 22, 23, and 24, it seems as though the sum of the first n integers is n(n+1)/2, that is, 1+2+3+ . . . +n = n(n+1)/2.

26. Let's have the program check this for us. Create another label on the form with the caption n*(n+1)/2.

27. Place a text box called txtCheck next to this label. See Figure 3.12 for the results.

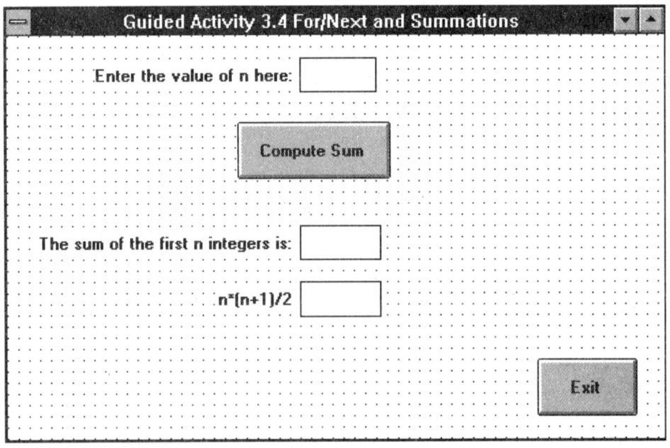

FIGURE 3.12
Modified user interface for Guided Activity 3.4

28. Open the Code window for cmdSum.

29. Add the following line immediately following txtSum.Text=Accum.

```
txtCheck.Text = n * (n + 1) / 2
```

30. Run the program again and enter several different values of n. Is the formula correct?

31. Exit Visual Basic and save as ga3-4.

Summations

To understand how the variable Accum in Guided Activity 3.4 accumulates the sum of the first n integers, let's trace the contents of the memory cell called Accum. After initializing Accum at 0, the contents of the cell would be as shown here.

In the loop, the initial value of i (1) is added to Accum. Thus, when the loop line is executed for the first time, Accum on the *right* has the value 0 and i is 1, so that Accum becomes 0 + 1 = 1. After execution, the cell Accum would contain 1, as shown.

The line Next i increments i to 2, and the loop line is executed again. This time Accum on the *right* is 1 and i is 2; therefore, Accum on the *left* side becomes 1 + 2 = 3, and 3 is stored in the memory cell Accum, as shown.

This process of adding the new value of i to the *old* value (the value of Accum on the right-hand side) to get the *new* total (the value of Accum on the left-hand side) continues until the loop is completed. At this point, the value of Accum will be the sum of the first n integers. This illustrates the standard method for doing a summation.

General Rules Concerning For/Next Loops

- The control variable may be used within the loop or it may not appear at all. However, be very careful not to change its value. This could cause the loop to go out of control or terminate prematurely.

- Every For statement must correspond exactly to one Next statement, each containing the same control variable.

- The initial, terminal, and incremental values can be variables, but cannot be changed within the loop.

- Be careful with the loop parameters such as the step size. The following would result in an infinite loop.

```
For N = 1 To 15 Step -1
```

With a negative increment, the control variable N would never reach the terminal value 15.

- The body of the loop for

```
For T = 15 To 1
```

would not be executed at all, since the control variable is initialized at a value greater than the terminal value. The addition of Step -1 would correct this problem.

Nested For/Next Loops

For/Next loops may be *nested*, that is, one loop or more loops stacked within another loop. If you use nested For/Next loops, the loops must not overlap. A loop may not be terminated before all the loops that lie within it are terminated. Thus, the termination of loops takes place from the *innermost* loop to the *outermost* loop. By way of illustration, the following loops are correct.

```
For I = 1 To 10
    For J = 1 To 10
        For K = 1 To 10
            Print I * J * K
        Next K
    Next J
Next I
```

But the following are incorrect.

```
For I = 1 To 10
    For J = 1 To 10
        X = I * J
        Print "The Product of "; I; "and"; J; " is "; X
        For K = 1 To 10
            Print K * X
        Next J
    Next K
Next I
```

The two inner loops overlap due to the misplaced Next statements; that is, the loop with control variable J overlaps the loop with control variable K, which is not permitted.

GUIDED ACTIVITY 3.5

Using a Nested For/Next Loop—A Multiplication Table

New features of Visual Basic contained in this activity:

- An event procedure for a text box
- More on formatting strings
- Height property
- Spc function
- Width property

The goal of this activity is to demonstrate nested loops by constructing a multiplication table.

1. Start Visual Basic.

2. Create the interface shown in Figure 3.13.

FIGURE 3.13
User interface for Guided Activity 3.5

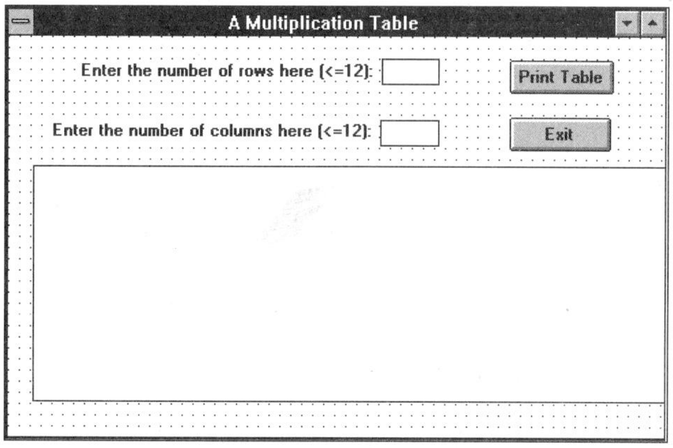

3. Change the caption to `A Multiplication Table` on the form.

4. Set the WindowState to 2-maximized.

5. Enter the usual code for the Exit button.

CHECKPOINT 3F   What is the code for an Exit button?

6. Set the following properties for the picture box.

Properties	Setting
FontName	Courier
Height	3000
Width	8500

NOTE *Height and width are given in twips where 1,440 twips equal one inch.*

7. Name the row text box txtRow.

8. Name the column text box txtCol.

9. Name the Print Table command button cmdPrTable and the Exit button cmdExit.

10. Enter the following code for the Print Table button.

```
picture1.Cls
picture1.Print Spc(3);
For Col = 1 To txtCol.Text
     picture1.Print Format$(Col, "@@"); Spc(2);
Next Col
picture1.Print
For Row = 1 To txtRow.Text
     picture1.Print Format$(Row, "@@");
     For Col = 1 To txtCol.Text
         picture1.Print Format$(Row * Col, "@@@"); Spc(1);
     Next Col
     picture1.Print
Next Row
txtRow.Text = ""
txtRow.SetFocus
```

11. Double-click the column text box.

12. Change the procedure to Click by clicking the arrow box at the right end of the Proc. box and selecting the event Click (the default event is Change).

13. Enter the following line of code into this event procedure.

```
txtCol.Text = ""
```

14. Set the tab indices as shown here.

Object	TabIndex
txtRow	0
txtCol	1
cmdPrTable	2
cmdExit	3

15. Click the Run icon on the toolbar.

16. To see a sevens multiplication table, enter 7 in the row text box.

17. Press [Tab] or click the column text box.

18. Enter 7 here.

19. Press [Tab] followed by [Enter] or click the Print Table button.

20. To see a twelves multiplication table, enter 12.

21. Press [Tab].

22. Enter another 12.

23. Press [Tab] followed by [Enter].

24. Try another table of your own choosing.

25. Save the project as ga3-5.

26. Exit Visual Basic.

About the New Features in Guided Activity 3.5

In the cmdPrTable_Click( ) procedure, we used the *Spc function* to help with the printing of the tables. The syntax for the function is Spc(*number*) where *number* specifies the number of blank or space characters that the Print method should print, starting at the current print position. The first print statement indents the column headings three spaces. Next, the column headings are separated by three spaces. The Print statement between the loops causes the Print method to advance to a new line after printing the column headings.

The *Height property* and the *Width property* determine the height and width of an object. We used them in Guided Activity 3.5 to ensure that the picture box was large enough for the multiplication table. For more information, consult the *Language Reference*.

The format character "@" (pronounced *at*) is used to print the rows and columns of the multiplication tables in neatly aligned rows and columns. It is used as a placeholder when formatting strings. If there is a character to be printed in the position corresponding to @, the character is printed; if not, a space is printed in that position. For more information on Spc and @, consult the *Language Reference*.

Finally, we used this activity to show that event procedures can also be associated with text boxes as well as command buttons. The purpose of this procedure is to clear the column text box when it is clicked to make it easier for the user to enter a new column value.

Keyword Syntax Review

Keyword—Syntax	Purpose
Do	To mark the start of a loop
Do Until (*condition true*)	To mark the start of a loop and to test the loop control variable
Do While (*condition true*)	To mark the start of a loop and to test the loop control variable
Loop Until (*condition true*)	To mark the end of a loop and to transfer control to Do
InputBox(*prompt*[,[*title*][,[*default*] [,*xpos,ypos*]]])	To display a prompt in a dialog box and to return a value input by the user to the program
Loop	To mark the end of a loop and to transfer control to the beginning of the loop
For *control variable = initial value* To *terminal value* [Step *increment*]	To mark the *start* of a For/Next loop
Next *control variable*	To mark the *end* of a For/Next loop
Or	A logical operator
Screen	To control the mouse pointer at run time
object.SetFocus	To set the focus of an *object*
Spc(*number*)	To skip the specified number of spaces
Tab(*column*)	To move to the specified column to print the next character

EXERCISE 3.1

Property Taxes

Property taxes are based on the assessed value of the property. The assessed value is a certain percentage of the fair market value. The property tax is a fixed amount per $100 of assessed value. For example, if the fair market value is $50,000 and the property is assessed at 25%, then the assessed value

$$Assessed\ Value = (Fair\ Market\ Value) * (Assessment\ Rate)$$
$$= (50000) * (.25) = 12500$$

If the rate per 100 of assessed value is $11.00, then the property tax is

$$Tax = (Assessed\ Value) / 100 * (Tax\ Rate\ Per\ 100)$$
$$= (A / 100) * (11) = 125 * 11 = 1375$$

Write an application using a loop to find the assessed value and the property tax for five properties. Input the fair market value using an InputBox. Assume that the assessment rate is 25%, and the tax rate is $11.00 per 100. Arrange the output to appear in text boxes as follows:

PROPERTY #1

ASSESSED VALUE $12,500.00

PROPERTY TAX $1,375.00

Run your program for the following data:

Property	Fair Market Value
1	50000
2	125000
3	250000
4	150000
5	94000

EXERCISE 3.2

Future Value of $1

Using an interface similar to Figure 3.10, write an application that will print a short table (similar to the one printed by tmptbl.mak saved in Guided Activity 3.4) of future values for $1 over a range of 10 periods based on an annual interest rate compounded monthly. The interest rate and the starting period are entered by the user through text boxes.

EXERCISE 3.3

Effective Interest Rates

The effective rate is the annual compound interest rate that will produce the same future value in one year as the annual rate J compounded K times a year. For J = 5% compounded monthly (K = 12) the effective rate is 5.116% or approximately 5.12%. Letting EFF be the effective rate, then EFF can be found for the formula

```
EFF = (1 + J / K) ^ K - 1
```

Write an application that outputs a two-column table of effective interest rates. The value of K and the starting value of J are to be entered through text boxes. The table should contain the effective rates from the starting rate to the starting rate plus 10% in steps of 0.5%.

EXERCISE 3.4

Sum of Squares

Using the application created in Guided Activity 3.4 as a model, write an application to find the sum of the first n squares $(1 + 2^2 + 3^2 + ... + n^2)$ for a value of n supplied by the user. Use your application to verify the formula $1 + 2^2 + 3^2 + ... + n^2 = [n (n + 1)(2n + 1)] / 6$.

EXERCISE 3.5

Sum of Cubes

Using the application created in Guided Activity 3.4 as a model, write an application to find the sum of the first n cubes $(1 + 2^3 + 3^3 + ... + n^3)$ for a value of n supplied by the user. Use your application to verify the formula $1 + 2^3 + 3^3 + ... + n^3 = [n (n + 1) / 2]^2$.

EXERCISE 3.6

Monthly Payments

The monthly payment on a loan is computed by using the formulas

$A = Rate * (1 + Rate) \verb|^| N$
$B = (1 + Rate) \verb|^| N - 1$
$Monthly\ Payment = Loan * A / B$

where *Rate* is the monthly interest rate, N is the number of months and *Loan* is the amount of the loan. A and B are just two intermediate values used to simplify the formula for *Monthly Payment*. Write an application to print a short table of monthly payments for ten different time periods in increments of six months. Permit the user to enter the starting number of months. Assume that the monthly interest rate is 1.25% and the amount of the loan is entered by the user. Arrange your output as follows:

AMOUNT OF LOAN: $1,000.00

# OF MONTHS	PAYMENT
12	$90.26
18	$62.38
ETC.	

Review Questions

1. What are relational expressions, and how are they used?

*2. The following procedure is supposed to print out the first 10 whole numbers together with their squares and cubes.

```
N = 1
Do Until N < 10
Form1.Print N, N * N, N * N * N
Loop
```

On the first run, nothing was printed. Why? Correct this problem. After correcting that problem, a second run produced an endless number of rows of 1's. Why? Correct this problem.

*3. When is a loop structure necessary in a program?

4. What is a pre-test loop?

*5. What is a post-test loop?

6. In what way is the Do Until/Loop combination different from the Do While/Loop combination?

7. What would be the exact output from the following procedure?

```
For K = 1 To 100
    For J = 1 To K
        Form1.Print "/"; " ";
    Next J
    Form1.Print " "
Next K
```

8. Find all of the errors in each of the following For/Next loops.

    a.
```
For J = 1 To 10 Step -1
    For K = 1 To J
        Form1.Print "*";
    Next J
    Form1.Print
Next K
```

Would this program segment, as given, run? What would be the output?

    b.
```
For I = 1 To 10
    For K = 1 To 10
        For I = 1 To 10
            Form1.Print I * K
        Next I
    Next K
Next I
```

9. What is the exact output from the following program segment?

```
For K = 1 To 5
    For L = 1 To K
        Form1.Print "*";
    Next L
    Form1.Print
Next K
```

10. Write a procedure using a For/Next or a Do Until loop to output the sequence 543210.

11. What is the output of the following For/Next loop?

```
For D = 20 To 10 Step 2
    Form1.Print D
Next D
```

*12. Write a For/Next loop to compute the sum of the odd whole numbers from 1 to 19.

*13. Consider the following For statement.

```
For Index = N ^ 2 To M + K Step 2 * N
```

How may times would the loop be executed if N = 2, M = 3, and K = 4?

*14. Is it permissible to assign a step value of zero in a For statement?

Important Terms

Argument	Logical operator	Relational operator
BackColor property	Loop	Screen object
Body of the loop	Loop control statement	SetFocus method
Boolean expression	Loop control variable	Spc function
Compound condition	Loop structure	String variable
Counter	Looping	Tab function
Digit placeholder	MousePointer property	Truth table
Endless loop	Nested	Truth value
Height property	Post-test structure	Width property
Infinite loop	Pre-test structure	
InputBox function	Relational expression	

Sequential Files

A convenient method for handling program data is to store it in a file on an auxiliary storage device such as a floppy disk or hard drive. When stored in a file, the same data is available to any number of programs, and data entry and modifications are made easier and more efficient. In this unit we study sequential files.

Learning Objectives

At the completion of this unit you should know

1. what a sequential file is,
2. how to open a sequential file,
3. how to close a sequential file,
4. how to read a sequential file,
5. how to write to a sequential file,
6. how to update a sequential file.

Important Keywords

Close

Dim

EOF

Input #

MsgBox

Open

Write #

Sequential Files

Up to this point, we have seen three ways of entering data:

- By using assignment statements

- By using text boxes

- By using the InputBox function

Assignment statements are fine for small amounts of data that do not change from run to run, but they are inconvenient when there are large quantities of data and/or frequent changes. A text box or the InputBox function do not handle large quantities of data any better, although they do make frequent changes easier to handle. Visual Basic provides another method of handling program data that overcomes the objections raised above.

A *sequential file* is a section of the external storage (such as a floppy disk or a hard drive) where data items are stored in a sequence, one data item immediately following another. Sequential files are easy to create and use. They also make efficient use of disk space. Two disadvantages are:

- An individual file item cannot be easily deleted or changed.

- To find a specific file item, it may be necessary to read a large portion of the file first.

A file is identified by a *file name* consisting of at most eight characters beginning with a letter and followed by an optional extension of at most three characters. The name and the extension are separated by a period. Extensions are used to identify the type of file. For instance, the extension .dat usually refers to a sequential data file, whereas .frm, or .mak, refers to a Visual Basic program file. Some examples are celfah.mak, or form1.frm.

NOTE *In this unit, from this point on, the word "file" is short for "sequential file."*

For example, consider the following file created using the Windows text editor Notepad.

```
Joe Doaks,125 South Street,Philadelphia,Pa.,19087(CR)(LF)
Sam Spade,2 North 5th Street,Lansdale,Pa.,10345(CR)(LF)
```

The notations (CR) and (LF) stand for a carriage return and a line feed that are generated by pressing [Enter] in Notepad. Actually, all of the data items could be entered on one line (provided there are no more than 256 characters). However, we have chosen to enter related data items on separate lines to make the file easier to read and edit. The individual data items are separated by commas, or a carriage return and a line feed.

The contents of a file may be thought of as a single column of data items with a **position pointer** (actually, the memory address of the next data item) that "points to" the next item to be processed. As the items are processed (written or read), the pointer automatically advances to the next item. For instance, the above file contents could be visualized as follows.

```
Joe Doaks              pointer
125 South Street
Philadelphia
Pa.
19087
Sam Spade
2 North 5th Street
Lansdale
Pa.
10345
```

File Operations

There are four file operations:

- Opening a file

- Closing a file

- Reading from a file

- Writing to a file

Opening a Sequential File

Before a file can be accessed, it must be opened.

The Open Statement—Syntax

Open *filename* For *mode* As [#] *filenumber*

For a sequential file there are three *file modes*—Input, Output, and Append. A file opened in the **Input mode** can be read, but not written to nor appended, and one opened in the **Output mode** can be written to, but not read nor appended. The **Append mode** is used to add new data to the end of a preexisting file. The *filenumber* is used in program code to refer to the file. The file name in an Open statement may be a variable, thus allowing the user to enter the file name at run time, and making it possible for the same program to process different data files.

Opening a file for *output* causes the computer to perform the following operations.

- The current directory is searched for the file name. If the file named already exists, the current contents will be lost as the new data is written into the file. If it does not already exist, the computer creates the file and enters its name into the directory.

- The computer sets aside a portion of memory called a **buffer**. This buffer is used to hold the data being written to the file. When the buffer is full (512 bytes), its contents are physically written to the disk.

- A file pointer is set at the beginning of the file. As the file is written, the pointer is updated so that it is always pointing at the current data item in the file.

- The file is assigned the file number given in the Open statement and is used by the program to communicate with the file. The file number may be any whole number from 1 to 255.

Opening a file for *input* requires the Open statement to perform the following tasks.

- The current directory is searched for the file name. If the name is found, the file is opened. If not, an error message is issued and the run is terminated.

- A portion of memory is set aside as a buffer.

- The file pointer is placed at the beginning of the file.

- The file number is assigned to the file.

The Open Statement—Examples

```
Open "Bank.dat" For Output As #1
Open "a:FNames.dat" For Input As #5
```

The first example opens a file called Bank.dat for output. The file number is the program link to the file. The program references the file by this number. The second example opens a file on drive A called FNames.dat as an input file identified as number 5. The Output mode creates a new file or opens an existing file and allows the computer to write data into it. In the case of a preexisting file, the computer rewrites it, destroying the previous contents. If you do not want the file rewritten, then the file should be opened in the Append mode. The Input mode opens the file so that its contents can be read into the computer's memory for processing.

Closing a File

Before exiting a program, all open files must be closed.

The Close Statement—Syntax

Close [[#]*filenumber*][,[#]*filenumber*] ...

The *filenumber* must agree with the number used in the corresponding Open statement. If no file number appears after Close, then *all* open files are closed.

The Close statement causes the computer to perform the following important tasks.

- Normally, the file buffer is emptied whenever it fills up. However, at the end of a run there may be data in the buffer that has not yet been written to the disk. In order not to lose this data, the Close statement writes it into a file on the disk.

- It writes an End Of File (EOF) marker into the file. This marker can be used by a program to determine when a file has been completely read.

- It frees the memory reserved for the buffer.

- It frees the file number for use by another file (or the same file) in another Open statement.

NOTE *Execution of an End statement automatically closes all open files. However, this method of closing files is not recommended and is considered poor programming technique.*

The Close Statement—Examples

Close #1

Close #2, #5, #6

Close

The first example closes file number 1. The second closes files numbered 2, 5, and 6. The last example is a blanket statement causing all open files to be closed regardless of number.

Before writing an application using a file, we introduce the built-in function EOF(n), which indicates when the end of a file has been reached. We'll use this function for loop control.

The EOF(n) Function—Syntax

EOF*(filenumber)*

As long as the end of the file has not been reached, EOF has the value zero. When the last data item in the file has been read, EOF takes the value -1, which indicates the end of the file has been reached.

The EOF(n) Function—Examples

Do Until EOF(100)

Do While EOF(2) <> -1

NOTE *The Close statement writes an end-of-file marker after the last data item written to the file.*

Reading from a File

To read data from a file, we use the Input # statement.

The Input # Statement—Syntax

Input # *filenumber, list of variables*

A comma is required between the *filenumber* and the list of variables that are to be read from the file.

The Input # Statement—Examples

```
Input #1, FName
Input #2, Shares, Cost, Value
```

The first example would read a single value into a Variant variable called FName from the file identified as file number 1. Similarly, the second example reads three values and assigns them to Shares, Cost, and Value in that order.

NOTE *The data in the file must be stored in an order compatible with the variable list in the Input # statement.*

A Payroll Application Illustrating How to Read a File

To illustrate the process of reading a sequential file, let's write a short payroll application. B&J TV Service Company has six employees who are paid by the hour. It is time to print the gross payroll for each employee and the total payroll for the week. The data for the week are shown here.

Employee	Hours	Rate
Schroff	72	15.00
Rich	42	13.50
Johnson	46	6.95
Adams	40	5.95
Mason	40	7.50
Keen	35.5	6.55

In the following, we assume that the above data (name, hours, and rate) for each employee are contained in a file called payrol.dat.

The following procedure will read the data from the file, compute the gross wages, figure the total payroll for the week, and print a table showing the employee name, the hours worked, the hourly rate, and the gross pay in four columns. We declare the data type for the employee's name as a string by attaching a dollar sign ($) to the right end of the name. This makes it clear that this variable is a string and not a number.

Code for the cmdPayRol Procedure

```
Sub cmdPayRol_Click ()
' Initialize the total payroll accumulator
Total = 0
Picture1.Print "Employee"; Tab(15); "Hours"; Tab(26); "Rate"; Tab(35);↲
      "Gross Pay"
Do Until EOF(1)
     Input #1, EmplName$, Hours, HrRate
     Wages = Hours * HrRate
     Total = Total + Wages
     Picture1.Print Tab(2); EmplName$; Tab(15); Hours; Tab(25); HrRate;↲
         Tab(35); Format$(Wages, "currency")
Loop
Picture1.Print "The Total Payroll for the Week is "; Format$(Total,↲
      "currency")
End Sub
```

Any code you want to be automatically executed at the beginning of a run, without any action on the part of the user, is placed in an event procedure called *Form_Load*. We use it to open the file payrol.dat.

Code for the Form_Load Procedure

```
Sub Form_Load ()
      Open "payrol.dat" For Input As #1
End Sub
```

We put the Close statement in the cmdExit_Click procedure.

Code for the cmdExit Procedure

```
Sub cmdExit_Click ()
     Close #1
     End
End Sub
```

GUIDED ACTIVITY 4.1

Reading a File

New features of Visual Basic contained in this activity:

- Closing a file

- EOF function

- Form_Load event procedure

- Input # statement

- String data type
- Using the Notepad editor
- Opening a file

In this activity you'll learn how to create a data file using Notepad, as well as how to open, read, and close a file. You also get to try out the Payroll Application.

1. Open the Accessories group in the Windows Program Manager.

2. Double-click the Notepad icon. Figure 4.1 shows the Notepad editor with the insertion point in the upper-left corner of the window.

FIGURE 4.1
Opening screen for Notepad

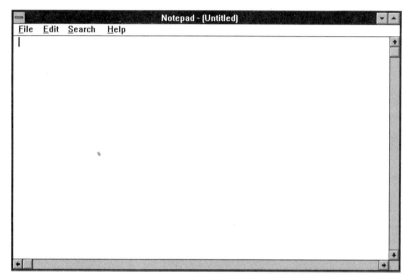

3. Enter the payroll data by typing, on separate lines, the name, hours, and rate separated by commas for each employee. Figure 4.2 shows the Notepad after the six lines of date have been entered.

4. Click the File title on the menu bar for Notepad.

5. Save the file as payrol.dat.

NOTE *Consult with your instructor as to where to save this file. You will probably want to save it on your student disk. If that is the case, save as* a:payrol.dat *(assuming your disk is in drive A). Another option would be to save in the Visual Basic directory, in which case, save it as* c:\vb\payrol.dat, *or change the disk and directory using the options in the Save As dialog box.*

6. Close Notepad and start Visual Basic.

7. Create the user interface using default properties as shown in Figure 4.3.

8. Change the caption and name of the Command1 button to Payroll and cmdPayRol, respectively.

FIGURE 4.2
Contents of the payrol.dat file

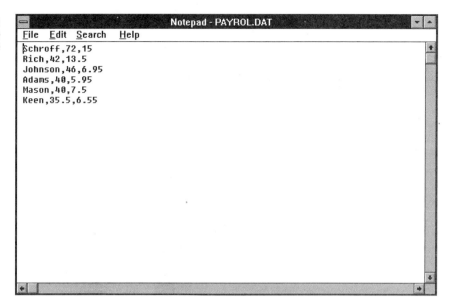

```
Notepad - PAYROL.DAT
File  Edit  Search  Help
Schroff,72,15
Rich,42,13.5
Johnson,46,6.95
Adams,40,5.95
Mason,40,7.5
Keen,35.5,6.55
```

9. Change the caption and name of the Command2 button to `Exit` and `cmdExit`, respectively.

10. Open the Project window by choosing Project from the drop-down menu under the Window title on the menu bar.

11. Select View Code from the Project window.

12. Click the arrow box next to the Object box.

13. Select cmdPayRol.

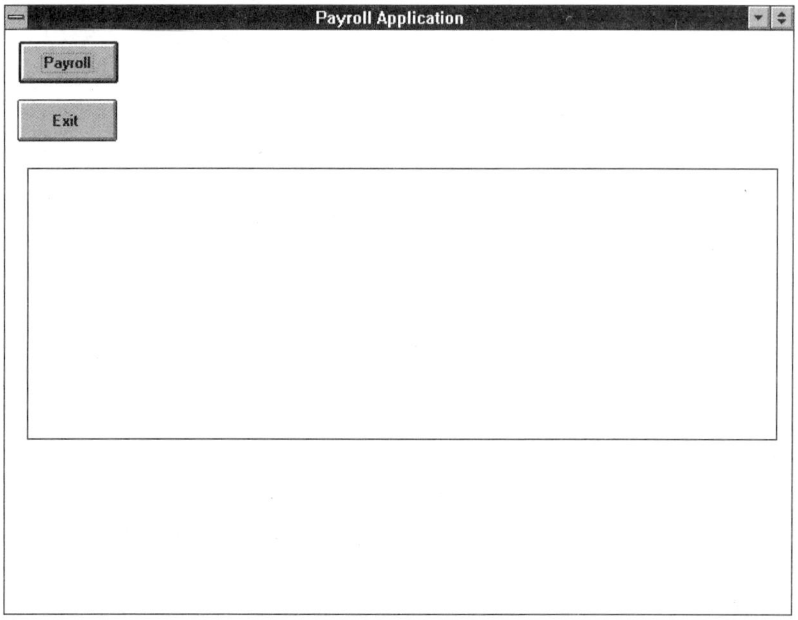

FIGURE 4.3
User interface for the Payroll Application

Payroll Application

Payroll

Exit

14. Enter the code given for this procedure.

15. Use the Object box to switch to the form.

16. Enter the code given for the Form_Load procedure.

17. Switch to cmdExit.

18. Enter the code given for this procedure.

19. Open the Project window.

20. Click View Form.

21. Open the Properties window and change the WindowState property to 2-Maximized and the caption to Payroll Application.

22. Click the Run icon.

23. Click the Payroll button. Figure 4.4 shows the output in the picture box.

FIGURE 4.4
Output of Payroll Application

```
Employee       Hours      Rate      Gross Pay
Schroff         72         15       $1,080.00
Rich            42         13.5     $567.00
Johnson         46         6.95     $319.70
Adams           40         5.95     $238.00
Mason           40         7.5      $300.00
Keen            35.5       6.55     $232.53
The Total Payroll for the Week is $2,737.23
```

24. Save the project as payrol by clicking the Save project icon on the toolbar.

CHECKPOINT 4A Which icon is the Save project icon?

25. Exit Visual Basic.

Writing to a File

Information can be written into a file by means of the Write # statement.

The Write # Statement—Syntax

Write # *filenumber*[, [*list of variables*]]

The Write # statement will not execute unless the file is open in the Output mode. The variable list may contain any combination of string and/or numeric expressions separated by commas or semicolons.

The Write # accomplishes the following tasks:

- It puts a comma between each item written to the file.

- It encloses each string item in quotation marks.

- It inserts a carriage return (CR) and a line feed (LF) at the end of each line written to the file.

The Write # Statement—Examples

```
Write #100, txtName.Text, Addr, State, Zip
Write #101, Apt; Street; IdNum; City
```

An Address Book Application Illustrating How to Write to a File

To illustrate writing to a file, let's write an address book application. With this application, the user will be able to create a personal address book.

We begin with the user interface shown in Figure 4.5.

FIGURE 4.5
User interface
for Address
Book Application

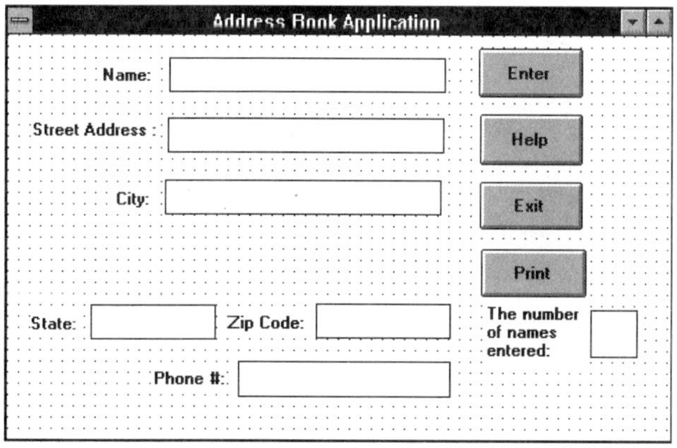

The user enters the information via six text boxes. After a name, address, and phone number have been entered, the user clicks the Enter button and the data is written to a file. The Help button provides information on how to use the program. When the last name and address have been entered, the program is stopped in the usual way by clicking the Exit button.

Here is the code for the three command buttons.

Code for the cmdHelp Procedure

```
Sub cmdHelp_Click ()
    Rem Define message for message box
    Part1 = "After entering all information in the spaces provided, ↵
        click Enter. "
    Part2 = "After entering the last name and address, click Enter ↵
        followed by Exit."
    Msg = Part1 & Part2
    MsgBox Msg
    txtName.SetFocus    ' Reset focus to Name text box
End Sub
```

We use the Help procedure to introduce *string concatenation* using the ampersand (&). We divided the message for the message box into two parts to make it easier to type in and to modify if necessary. The ampersand concatenates (links) the two strings into one continuous string denoted by Msg. To display Msg on the screen, we use the MsgBox statement.

The MsgBox Statement—Syntax

```
MsgBox msg [,[type][,title]]
```

The message displayed in the dialog box generated by this statement is contained in the string expression *msg*. The optional value of the numeric expression *type* determines what is displayed in the dialog box along with the message. The optional string expression *title* is displayed in the title bar of the box. For more information on the MsgBox, consult the *Language Reference*.

When this statement is executed, Msg is displayed in a box as shown in Figure 4.6. The user must respond by clicking OK or by pressing Enter.

Code for the cmdEnter Procedure

```
Sub cmdEnter_Click ()
    Write #100, txtName.Text, txtAddress.Text, txtCity.Text, ↵
        txtState.Text, txtZip.Text, txtPhone.Text
    n = n + 1
    txtCount.Text = n
    Rem Prepare text boxes for next name and address
    txtName.Text = "" : txtAddress.Text = ""
    txtCity.Text = "": txtState.Text = "": txtZip.Text = "": ↵
        txtPhone.Text = ""
    txtName.SetFocus
End Sub
```

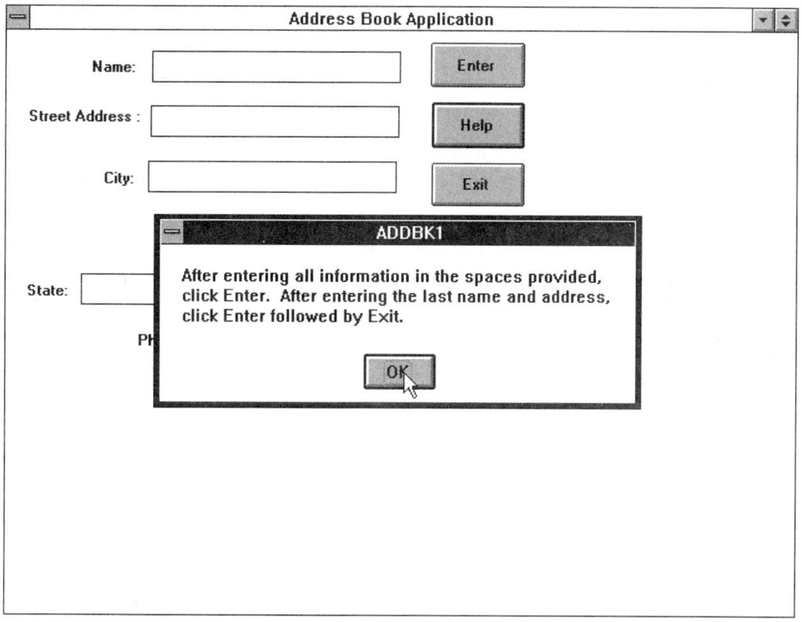

FIGURE 4.6
Message box displayed by the Help button

```
┌─────────────────────────────────────────────────────┐
│ ─         Address Book Application            ▼ ▲    │
│                                                       │
│   Name:  [                    ]      ┌─────┐          │
│                                      │Enter│          │
│  Street Address : [             ]    └─────┘          │
│                                      ┌─────┐          │
│   City: [                    ]       │Help │          │
│                                      └─────┘          │
│                                      ┌─────┐          │
│                                      │Exit │          │
│              ┌──────── ADDBK1 ────────┐               │
│   State: [   │ After entering all information in the  │
│              │ spaces provided, click Enter. After    │
│          P   │ entering the last name and address,    │
│              │ click Enter followed by Exit.          │
│              │            ┌────┐                      │
│              │            │ OK │                      │
│              │            └────┘                      │
│              └────────────────────────┘               │
└─────────────────────────────────────────────────────┘
```

NOTE *The Write # statement is one line when entered into the program, but is shown here on two lines.*

There are several new features of Visual Basic introduced through this procedure. Each time the Enter button is clicked, this procedure is executed from the beginning. That would mean that the variable n would start over at zero. That is, n would be considered by Visual Basic to be a *local variable* having meaning only in this procedure. To do the count correctly, we need n to be considered a *module-level variable* so that the value of n will be retained from one procedure call to the next for the entire run, not reset to 0 (zero) each time the procedure is executed. This is accomplished by declaring n as an integer variable within the *general object*. The general object is a special section of the form used for things other than objects. You will find this object listed as (general) in the Object box when you select View Code in the Project window. When (general) is selected, the Proc box reads (declarations). This is where you declare variables you want to be module-level. These declarations are done by means of Dim statements. A module-level variable is available to every procedure in the form.

The Dim Statement—Syntax

Dim *variable name* [As *type*] [,*variable name* [As *type*]]

What the Dim statement does is declare a variable, that is, identify a certain character string as a variable. It can also be used to declare a variable's type such as Integer, as we intend to do in this application. By declaring a variable as an integer, the computer allocates two bytes of memory for this variable, thus limiting its value to an integer between -32,768 and 32,767. This is the second variable type we have seen. The first was the Variant type. We'll be introducing others later. For more information on variable types consult the *Language Reference*.

The following line is the only line in the (general) object.

Code for the (general) Object

```
Dim n As Integer
```

We open the file and initialize n in the Form_Load procedure.

Code for the Form_Load Procedure

```
Sub Form_Load ()
      Open "addbook.dat" For Output As #100
      n = 0
End Sub
```

Finally, the Exit procedure.

Code for the cmdExit Procedure

```
Sub cmdExit_Click ()
      Close #100
      End
End Sub
```

GUIDED ACTIVITY 4.2

Writing to a File

New features of Visual Basic contained in this activity:

- Dim statement
- General object
- Integer data type
- Module-level variable
- MsgBox statement
- String concatenation

This activity demonstrates how a sequential file is written by the **Address Book** Application.

1. Start Visual Basic.

2. Create the user interface as shown in Figure 4.5.

3. Enter the property settings using Figure 4.5.

4. Set the text box names according to the cmdEnter procedure.

5. Enter the code for the command button cmdEnter.

6. Enter the code for the command button cmdHelp.

7. Enter the code for the command button cmdExit.

8. Enter the Dim statement in the (general) object.

CHECKPOINT 4B What is the purpose of the Dim statement in this program?

9. Click the Run icon on the toolbar.

10. Click the Help button.

11. Click OK.

12. Enter the following data in the appropriate boxes. Be sure to click Enter after each line.

```
Joe Doaks, 125 South Street, Philadelphia, Pa., 19087, 201-555-1234
Sam Spade, 2 North 5th Street, Lansdale, Pa., 19870, 610-555-3412
The Shadow, 123 Anywhere, Hollywood, Calif., 32456, 701-324-1243
```

13. Stop the run by clicking the Exit button.

14. Click the Window Control Menu box in the upper-left corner of the Visual Basic window.

15. Select the Switch to command.

16. Click the Program Manager.

17. Double-click the Accessories icon.

18. Open Notepad.

19. Open file c:\vb\addbook.dat to see the contents of the file just written, as shown in Figure 4.7.

20. Close Notepad.

21. Click the Window Control Menu box in the Program Manager and switch back to Visual Basic.

22. Save the form as addbk.frm and the project as addbk.mak.

23. Exit Visual Basic.

An Application to Add Items to a File

Suppose we want to add some more names to our address book. A slight modification of the Address Book Application will make this possible. The only line we need to change is the Open statement in the Form_Load procedure. We simply change it from the Output mode to the Append mode as shown here.

```
Open "addbook.dat" For Append As #100
```

FIGURE 4.7
Contents of
addbook.dat file
after run

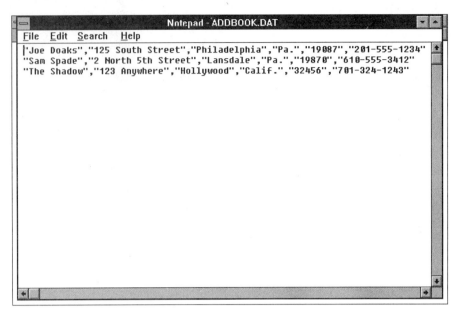

GUIDED ACTIVITY 4.3

Appending a File

New features of Visual Basic contained in this activity:

- Append mode
- Variable file name

In this activity we show how a file name can be entered by the user at run time and how data can be added to an existing file.

1. Start Visual Basic.

2. Open the addbk.mak project.

3. View the code in the Form_Load procedure.

CHECKPOINT 4C What is the quickest way to view the code attached to a particular object?

4. Add the following two lines as the *first* two lines of code.

```
Prompt = "Please enter the name of the address book file. Then click OK"
FName = InputBox$(Prompt)
```

5. Change the Open statement to the following:

```
Open FName For Append As #100
```

6. Click the Run icon.

CHECKPOINT 4D What are some of the other ways to start a run?

7. Enter addbook.dat in the input box.

8. Click OK.

9. Add the following two names and addresses to the file.

    ```
    Jessica Johnson, 35 Wicklow Drive, Tabernacle, N.J., 08034, 201-555-1234
    Deborah Barron, 7548 Sunset Drive, Avalon, N.J., 08202, 201-555-4321
    ```

10. Stop the run by clicking Exit.

11. Switch to the Program Manager.

12. Start Notepad.

13. Open addbook.dat and observe that the two new names now appear at the end of the file.

14. Exit Notepad.

15. Switch to Visual Basic.

16. Use the Save As command and save the project as `addbkapp.mak`.

17. Exit Visual Basic.

Keyword Syntax Review

Keyword—Syntax	Purpose
Close [[#]*filenumber*][,[#]*filenumber*] ...	To close the files corresponding to the numbers
EOF(*filenumber*)	To determine if the end of the file has been reached
Input #*filenumber, list of variables*	To read data from a file
MsgBox *msg* [,[*type*][,*title*]]	To provide information for the user
Open *filename* For *mode* As [#] *filenumber*	To open a file in the given mode and with the given number
Write #*filenumber* [,[*list of variables*]	To write data to a file

EXERCISE 4.1

Payroll

1. Using the payroll example in the text as a model, write a procedure to print the following information and column headings for a payroll statement.

    ```
    B&J TV Service

    Payroll for the week of December 19, 1994

    Employee      Hours      Hourly    Gross                      Net
    Name          Worked     Wage      Salary    Deductions       Pay
    ```

2. Employees of B&J TV are paid by the hour. Each employee has a certain percentage of his or her gross pay deducted for taxes. Using a file for data entry, modify the procedure you wrote for part 1 of this exercise to produce a table containing six columns with the given headings. Each line of the data file should contain the employee's name, # of hours worked, hourly rate, and % deduction. The relevant formulas are:

*Gross = Hours * Rate*
*Deductions = (% Deduction / 100) * (Gross)*
Net pay = Gross - Deductions

Test your program with the following data.

```
Adams, 40, 15.5, 28
Bates, 42, 10.5, 19
Cates, 35, 13.5, 28
Jones, 40, 7.5, 19
Leahy, 52.5, 12.5, 36
Monty, 65.75, 25.25, 36
```

3. After designing a user interface, write an application to output the payroll statement using the procedure you wrote in parts 1 and 2.

EXERCISE 4.2

Bank Statement

1. Write a procedure to print a heading for a bank statement in a picture box as shown here.

```
                  Last National Bank
              Statement for December 1994
                Account #: 1234-56-7890

John H. Smithe
321 Pine Circle
Pinecrest, Vt. 12345
```

2. Modify the procedure you wrote for part 1 to add the following list of transactions to the bank statement.

Transaction	Balance
Opening	$100.00
($23.75)	$76.25
($10.40)	$65.85
($50.00)	$115.85
($7.25)	$108.60
($42.50)	$66.10
($22.85)	$43.25
$40.00	$83.25

```
($50.33)            $32.92
$66.75              $99.67
THE LAST NUMBER IN THE SECOND COLUMN IS THE CLOSING BALANCE.
```

Use Notepad to create a file called `trans.dat` containing the transactions shown in the Transaction column. The entries in parentheses are negative and represent checks. Use the "currency" format string to format the output, which outputs negative values in parentheses. Your data consists of the opening balance plus all the transactions found in the Transaction column. A positive value is a deposit. The first number in the data is the initial balance. Be sure to document your program.

3. After designing a user interface, write an application to output the payroll statement using the procedure you wrote in parts 1 and 2.

EXERCISE 4.3

Table of Equivalent Speeds

Write an application that reads the number of miles per hour from a file and converts it to feet per second and kilometers per hour. Your output should be in tabular form as shown below. To convert miles per hour to feet per second, multiply the miles per hour by 1.4667. To convert feet per second to kilometers per hour, multiply the feet per second by 1.09728. All output should be expressed to the nearest whole number. Test your program with the following miles per hour: 10, 15, 20, 25, 30, 40, 50, 55, 60. Format your output as shown:

```
              Table of Equivalent Speeds

    Miles            Feet          Kilometers
     Per             Per              Per
    Hour            Second            Hour

     10              15               16
     15              22               24
     20              29               32
     25              37               41
      .               .                .
      .               .                .
      .               .                .
     60              88               97
```

EXERCISE 4.4

Electric Bills

The following are the average costs per hour to run certain electrical appliances and the average number of hours used per month.

```
12 cu ft refrigerator    $0.0091        360
15 cu ft freezer          0.0158        375
toaster                   0.09          5
hair dryer                0.15          7.5
color TV                  0.0333        180
```

Write an application that reads the name of the appliance, the average cost factors, and the total number of hours of usage for the month from a file and prints the following report.

```
Appliance                Total Hours      Cost
12 Cu Ft Refrigerator        360         $3.28
Etc.

                              Total    $16.77
                              Tax:       .40
```

The federal tax rate is 2.38% of the total bill. Have the total printed at the end of the last column and the tax printed as a separate item as shown.

EXERCISE 4.5

Future Value and Compound Interest

Design an appropriate interface and write an application to produce a table showing the principal, rate, frequency of conversion, number of periods, the future value, and the compound interest. Enter the following data into a file and use it to test your program.

Principal	Rate	Frequency	#of periods
$2000	6%	12	6
750	5.25	4	20
1050	5.5	12	25
20000	14.3	365	180

Your output should be as follows.

Principal	Rate	Frequency	#of periods	Future Value	Interest
$2000.00	6%	12	6	$2,060.76	$60.76
750.00	5.25%	4	20	$973.47	$223.47
1050	5.5%	12	25	$1,177.17	$127.17
20000	14.3%	365	180	$21,461.04	$1,461.04

Review Questions

1. The data items are stored in a file in a _____.

2. What are the four file operations?

*3. A file may be opened for _____, _____, or _____.

4. What is the purpose of the Open statement?

*5. What is the purpose of the Close statement?

6. What is an End of File marker?

7. What is a file position pointer?

*8. What statement is used to read a file?

9. What statement is used to write information into a file?

10. What is a buffer?

11. What file mode permits the new information to be added to an existing file?

*12. What is the link between a file and the program code?
    # assigned   to the file by the open statement

Important Terms

Append mode	General object	Output mode
Buffer	Input mode	Position pointer
File mode	Local variable	Sequential file
Form_Load	Module-level variable	String concatenation

Decision Structures

This unit completes our introduction to Visual Basic programming and our study of the three fundamental control structures—sequence, loop, and decision. These three structures are the only structures required to write any program. In this unit we study the decision structure.

Learning Objectives

At the completion of this unit you should know

1. the three types of decision structures,
2. the general syntax of the block If/Then statement,
3. the general syntax of the block If/Then/Else statement,
4. how to use the logical operators And and Not,
5. the truth tables for And and Not,
6. how to use a frame,
7. how to use option buttons,
8. how logic statements are evaluated according to the logical operator hierarchy,
9. how to diagram a compound condition to find its truth value,
10. how to use the Int function,
11. how to use the Mod operator,
12. the general syntax for the Select Case statement.

Important Keywords

And

Case

Else

EndIf

Exit

If

Int

LCase$

Mod

Not

Select

Then

UCase$

The Single Option Block If/Then Statement

The computer sometimes needs to make decisions. Visual Basic provides three types of *decision structures*—the *single option decision structure*, the *dual option decision structure*, and the *multioption decision structure*. First, we take a look at the single option structure.

A flowchart for this structure is shown in Figure 5.1.

FIGURE 5.1
A flowchart for the single option block If/Then statement

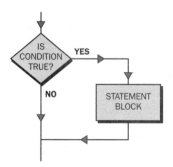

The Single Option Block If/Then Statement—Syntax

```
If (condition) Then
    [statement block]
End If
```

If the condition is true, then the statement block following Then is executed. If it is false, the statement following End If is executed.

A Ticket Pricing Procedure Illustrating the Single Option Block If/Then Statement

The block If/Then statement is in boldface.

```
Sub cmdCompPrice_Click ()
Rem   Ticket Pricing Application
Rem   This procedure determines the price per ticket for a
Rem   bus tour and the total revenue due the bus company.
Rem   If 100 or more sign up for the tour, a 15% price reduction
Rem   is given per ticket.
Rem   Variable List:
Rem      Ticket = Number of tickets sold
Rem       Price = Price per ticket
Picture1.Cls: Picture2.Cls
Price = 120
Tickets = txtTickets.Text
If Tickets >= 100 Then
     Price = .85 * Price
End If
Picture1.Print Format$(Price, "currency")
Picture2.Print Format$(Price * Tickets, "currency")
txtTickets.Text = ""
txtTickets.SetFocus
End Sub
```

It is clear from the above code that the number of tickets is entered through a text box. If the number of tickets is greater than or equal to 100, the statement following Then is executed, which lowers the price of a ticket by 15%. Otherwise, the price remains at $120. The last two lines of the procedure clear the contents of the ticket text box and give it the focus. This makes it convenient for the user to enter a new number of tickets.

To further illustrate the If/Then statement, we enhance the ticket pricing application by adding some new objects to the form. The first is called a *frame*. A frame acts like a container to hold other controls. In this case we want to use it to hold another new object called an *option button*. An option button is used to display a choice that can be selected by the user. The *Value property* of an option button has a Boolean value of "True" or "False." If the Value is "True," the button has been selected; if "False," it has not been selected. When the Value is "True," we say the button is "on," and when "False," it is considered to be "off."

For this application, we place three option buttons in the frame to allow the user to choose a destination city. Each city has its own base ticket price that is set when the given city is selected by its option button. Since the three buttons are in a frame, they are treated as a group of objects that can be moved around the form as a unit. In addition, when an option button is turned on within the frame, the other option buttons are automatically turned off. Thus, a user can only select one option button within a group. The frame must be created *first* and then the option buttons are drawn inside. Otherwise, the buttons will not move with the frame.

Figure 5.2 shows the interface we will be using for the ticket pricing application.

Next, we list the code for the three option buttons.

Code for the optAtlCty Procedure

```
Sub optAtlCty_Click ()
If optAtlCty.Value = True Then
    Price = 95
End If
End Sub
```

Code for the optNewYork Procedure

```
Sub optNewYork_Click ()
If optNewYork.Value = True Then
    Price = 165
End If
End Sub
```

Code for the optPhil Procedure

```
Sub optPhil_Click ()
If optPhil.Value = True Then
    Price = 120
End If
End Sub
```

Since the value of the variable Price is coming from one of the three options, we need to delete the line in cmdCompPrice that sets the value at 120. In addition, the variable Price must be a module-level variable. Consequently, we add the following line to the (general) object.

```
Dim Price As Single
```

This line declares Price as a variable of data type *Single*, which means that Price is a 4-byte *floating point* (contains a decimal point) number or a *real* number in the range from -3.402823E38 to -1.401298E-45 if negative, and from 1.401298E-45 to 3.402823E38 if positive. We did this because Price contains a decimal point. We could also have simply declared it without a data type. In this case, it would be assigned as a Variant data type (the default data type). That would have worked equally well.

The following Guided Activity gives you a chance try out what we just explained.

GUIDED ACTIVITY 5.1

Using the Ticket Pricing Application

New features of Visual Basic contained in this activity:

- Frame object
- Option button
- Single data type
- Value property

In this activity you get to try out the Ticket Pricing Application and to see how option buttons work.

1. Start Visual Basic.
2. Click the Frame icon in the Toolbox. It is the third icon in the left-hand column.
3. Place the frame in the position shown in Figure 5.2.
4. Open the Properties window.

CHECKPOINT 5A What function key opens the Properties window?

5. Set the Caption property for the frame to Pick a destination.
6. Click the Option Button icon in the Toolbox. It is the fourth icon in the right-hand column.
7. Draw the option button Option1 in the frame.
8. Open the Properties window and set the caption to Atlantic City.
9. Repeat steps 6, 7, and 8 for the second option button captioned New York.
10. Repeat steps 6, 7, and 8 for the third option button captioned Philadelphia.
11. Change the names of the three option buttons to optAtlCty, optNewYork, and optPhil, respectively.
12. Create the rest of the interface. Use the cmdCompPrice procedure to obtain the settings.
13. Double-click the first option button (Atlantic City).
14. Enter the code for the optAtlCty Click procedure.
15. Repeat steps 13 and 14 for the other two option buttons.

16. Double-click the Compute Price button.

17. Enter the code for the cmdCompPrice Click procedure.

18. Delete the line that assigns the value of Price as 120. To delete a line, place the cursor on the line and press [Ctrl][Y] or highlight the line and press [Del].

19. Enter the usual code for the Exit button.

20. Enter the following line in the (general) object.

    ```
    Dim Price As Single
    ```

21. Start a run.

22. Enter 50 for the number of tickets.

23. Click the Philadelphia option button.

CHECKPOINT 5B   Is there any way to select Philadelphia without using the mouse?

24. Click the Compute Price button. The price per ticket should be $120.00 and the total revenue $6,000.00.

25. Enter 100 for the number of tickets.

26. Click the Atlantic City option button.

27. Click the Compute Price button. The price per ticket should be $80.75 and the total revenue $8,075.00.

28. Let's see what happens if you click the Compute Price button *without* entering a number in the txtTickets box. Click the Compute Price button. Visual Basic displays a type mismatch error message because nothing—that is, a blank—was present in the txtTickets box.

29. Click OK in the message box.

30. Click the down arrow in the upper-right corner of the window so that the Stop run icon becomes visible (assuming the form window is maximized).

31. Click the Stop run icon on the toolbar.

32. Restart the run.

33. Enter 50 for the number of tickets.

34. Click the Compute Price button *without* choosing a destination. Note that $0.00 appears in both picture boxes. This is because no destination was chosen and, therefore, Price = 0 by default.

35. To continue, reenter 50 for the number of tickets and select Atlantic City for the destination.

36. Click the Compute Price button. Everything should be correct now.

37. Click Exit.

38. Save the project as tickpr1.

39. Exit Visual Basic.

Error Checking

As we saw at the end of Guided Activity 5.1, things can get confusing when the user fails to enter a number of tickets or forgets to choose a destination. As the programmer, you need to anticipate user mistakes. Whenever the user clicks the Compute Price button, we need to check for two things. First, was a number entered in the text box, and, second, was a destination chosen?

Let's consider the first case. If no number was entered for the number of tickets, then txtTickets.Text will be a blank. In such a case, we use a message box to inform the user. The user will then click the OK button in the message box. At this point, we reset the focus to the text box so that a number can be entered. We also need to do one other thing. Since no number of tickets was entered, we do not want to continue with the procedure. To exit the procedure before it is complete, we use the Exit Sub statement. When this statement is executed, the procedure is terminated just as it would be if the End Sub statement had been executed.

The code to handle a missing number of tickets is shown next.

```
If Tickets = "" Then
    Msg = "You must enter the number of tickets needed before clicking ↵
        Compute Price"
    MsgBox Msg, 16, "Ticket Pricing"
    txtTickets.SetFocus
    Exit Sub
End If
```

NOTE *The type 16 in the message box statement causes a red stop sign to be shown as part of the message box display. For other type choices, consult the* Language Reference.

Now, let's deal with the missing destination. If no destination has been selected, then the Value property for each of the option buttons will be False. To check if this is the case, we use the logical operator And. A compound condition statement using And is True, if and only if *all* component conditions are true. To check if a destination has been entered, we use the code shown here.

```
If optPhil.Value = False And optAtlCty.Value = False And ↵
        optNewYork.Value = False Then
    Msg = "You must pick a destination"
    MsgBox Msg, 16, "Ticket Pricing"
    Exit Sub
End If
```

Thus, for the condition

```
optPhil.Value = False And optAtlCty.Value = False And ↵
    optNewYork.Value = False
```

to have the value of True, each component must be true, that is, the Value property of each option button must be False.

GUIDED ACTIVITY 5.2

Adding Error Checking to the Ticket Pricing Application

New features of Visual Basic contained in this activity:

- And operator
- Error trapping
- Exit Sub

In this activity you'll learn how to trap user errors and to keep the application running.

1. Start Visual Basic.

2. Open the tickpr1.mak project.

3. Open the Code window for cmdCompPrice.

4. Enter the two error checking blocks of code between the lines

   ```
   Tickets = txtTickets.Text
   ```
   and
   ```
   If Tickets <= 100 Then
   ```

5. Start a run.

6. Click the Compute Price button without entering a number of tickets.

7. Click OK.

8. Enter 50 for the number of tickets.

9. Click the Compute Price button *without* entering a destination.

10. Click OK.

11. Click Atlantic City.

12. Click the Compute Price button.

13. Try a few other examples of your own choosing.

14. Using the Save As command, save the form and the project as tickpr2.

15. Exit Visual Basic.

The Dual Option Block If/Then/Else Statement

Suppose B&J TV (from Unit 4) decides to pay time-and-a-half for each hour over 40 per week. Thus, an employee receives the hourly rate for the first 40 hours and one-and-a-half times this rate for each hour over 40. This leads to two ways of finding the gross pay Wages depending on how Hours compares with 40. For Hours less than or equal to 40 we use Wages = Hours * HrRate, and for Hours greater than 40 we use Wages = 40 * HrRate + (Hours – 40) * 1.5 * HrRate. In this formula, (Hours – 40) is the number of hours over 40 and 1.5 * HrRate is the hourly rate increased by 50% or one-and-a-half times the normal hourly rate. When there is overtime, the gross pay equals 40 hours at the normal rate plus the overtime represented by the second part of the formula.

The Block If/Then/Else Statement

Having two formulas for Wages means that the computer needs the ability to make a choice between two options. Dual option decision making is implemented by means of the block If/Then/Else statement. We begin by first drawing a flowchart to show the options of our new program, as illustrated in Figure 5.3.

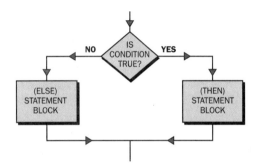

FIGURE 5.3
A flowchart for the dual option block If/Then/Else statement

The Dual Option Block If/Then/Else Statement—Syntax

```
If (condition) Then
    [statement block]
Else
    [statement block]
End If
```

If and Then must appear on the same line with nothing following Then. Else must be on a line by itself. All block If/Then/Else statements must conclude with an End If on a separate line. Any number of Visual Basic statements can be used between If/Then and Else. Likewise between Else and the pair End If. When the condition has a truth value of True, the computer executes the lines following Then, branches over the Else statement to the End If, and continues the run from there. A truth value of False causes the computer to branch over the Then statements and execute the statements following Else to the End If. In any case, only one set of statements is carried out.

Specifically, we need to change the way the wages are computed in the Payroll Application of Unit 4 in order to implement payment for overtime. First, let's recall how the wages were computed in that application. Here is the relevant portion of the cmdPayRol procedure.

```
Do Until EOF(1)
    Input #1, EmplName$, Hours, HrRate
    Wages = Hours * HrRate
```

```
      Total = Total + Wages
      Picture1.Print Tab(2); EmplName$; Tab(15); Hours; Tab(25); ↵
         HrRate;  Tab(35); Format$(Wages, "currency")
      Picture1.Print
Loop
```

To change the way the wages are computed, we replace the line

```
Wages = Hours * HrRate
```

with a block If/Then/Else statement.

```
If Hours <= 40 Then
     Wages = Hours * HrRate
Else
     Wages = 40 * HrRate + (Hours - 40) * 1.5 * HrRate
End If
```

This statement block executes in the following manner. First, the condition Hours <= 40 is tested. If it is true, then Wages = Hours * HrRate is carried out and the statement following Else is ignored. The computer then moves on to the next line following the End If statement and continues the run. On the other hand, if it is false, then the statement following the word Else is executed and the one following Then is ignored. And, as before, the run then continues with the next line following End If.

The new procedure is shown here.

Code for the Revised cmdPayRol Procedure

```
Sub cmdPayRol_Click ()
' Initialize the total payroll accumulator
Total = 0
picture1.Print "Employee"; Tab(15); "Hours"; Tab(26); "Rate"; ↵
     Tab(35); "Gross Pay"
Do Until EOF(1)
     Input #1, EmplName$, Hours, HrRate
     If Hours <= 40 Then
        Wages = Hours * HrRate
     Else
        Wages = 40 * HrRate + (Hours - 40) * 1.5 * HrRate
     End If
     Total = Total + Wages

     picture1.Print Tab(2); EmplName$; Tab(15); Hours; Tab(25); ↵
        HrRate; Tab(35); Format$(Wages, "currency")
     picture1.Print
Loop
picture1.Print "The Total Payroll for the Week is "; Format$(Total, ↵
     "currency")
End Sub
```

Here is a run of the revised procedure using the same data as before.

Employee	Hours	Rate	Gross Pay
Schroff	72	15	$1320.00
Rich	42	13.5	$580.50
Johnson	46	6.95	$340.55
Adams	40	5.95	$238.00
Mason	40	7.5	$300.00
Keen	35.5	6.55	$232.53

The Total Payroll for the Week is $3,011.58

Logical Operators

Up to now, we have used the relational operators (=, <, >, <=, >=, < >) and the logical operators Or and And to write the conditions controlling the loops and decisions. Let's review the operator Or.

The Or Logical Operator

A compound condition using Or is true if, and only if, *at least* one of the component conditions is true. The compound condition

```
If Mer = "PM" Or TOD > 12 THEN
      Print "It is afternoon"
End If
```

evaluates as true *if* Mer = "PM" *or* TOD > 12 is true *or* if both are true. It is false *only if* both conditions, Mer = "PM" and TOD > 12, are false. See Table 5.1.

TABLE 5.1 *Truth table for the logical operator Or*		

CONDITION 1	CONDITION 2	CONDITION 1 OR CONDITION 2
true	true	true
true	false	true
false	true	true
false	false	false

The And Logical Operator

A compound condition using And is true if, and only if, all component conditions are true. For example, the compound condition in

```
If NMonth = "April" And Day = 15 Then
      Print "Taxes are due!"
End If
```

will evaluate as true *only* if NMonth = "April" *and* Day = 15 are *both* true. If either one is false, the compound condition is false and the Then clause is ignored. See Table 5.2.

	CONDITION 1	CONDITION 2	CONDITION 1 OR CONDITION 2
TABLE 5.2 *Truth table for the logical operator And*	true	true	true
	true	false	false
	false	true	false
	false	false	false

The Not Logical Operator

The logical operator Not is an **unary operator** (has only one operand) used to negate a single expression. That is, Not reverses the truth value of an expression—a true condition becomes false and a false condition becomes true. A relational expression preceded by the Not operator forms a condition that is *true* when the relational expression is *false* and *false* when the relational expression is *true*. In other words, Not negates the truth value of the expression it precedes. Consider the condition in

```
If Not (Mer = "PM") Then
     Print "It is morning"
End If
```

which is *true* when Mer = "PM" is *false*. It follows that if Mer = "AM," then "It is morning" will be printed. On the other hand, if Mer = "PM" is true, then Not (Mer = "PM") is false and the Then clause will be ignored. See Table 5.3.

	CONDITION	NOCONDITION2
TABLE 5.3 *Truth table for the logical operator Not*	true	false
	false	true

Combining And, Or, and Not

Just as there is a hierarchy for arithmetic operators, there is also a hierarchy for logical operators. In a compound condition, working from left to right, conditions containing relational expressions are evaluated first, followed by those containing Not operators, then by those containing And operators, and lastly by those conditions containing Or operators. Parentheses can be used to interrupt this order of evaluation. The hierarchy of all operators is summarized in Table 5.4.

To illustrate operator hierarchy let's consider some compound conditions.

```
If (yr < 90 And yr >= 80) Or cent < 1900 Then
     Print "The year is in the 80's or it is the 20th century."
End If
```

TABLE 5.4	OPERATOR	OPERATION
Operator hierarchy	^	Exponentiation
	Unary plus or minus	Sign assignment
	*, /	Multiplication and division
	+, −	Addition and subtraction
	=, <, >, <=, >=, <>	Relational
	Not	Negation
	And	Logical connection
	Or	Logical connection

Following the order of evaluation outlined in Table 5.4 and taking into account the parentheses around the first condition, this condition would be evaluated as follows. First, the truth value of (yr < 90 And yr >= 80) is determined, then the truth value of the Or statement. Suppose yr = 85 and cent = 1900, then the condition (yr < 90 And yr >= 80) would be true (according to Table 5.2) and cent < 1900 would be false. According to Table 5.1, the compound condition would be true and the Then clause would be executed.

This evaluation can be diagrammed as follows, assuming yr = 85 and cent = 1900.

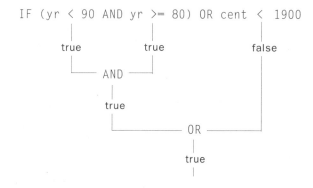

Let's diagram the case where yr = 79 and cent = 1900.

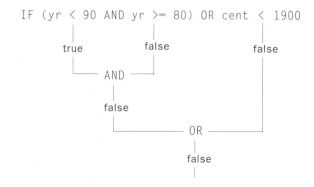

In this case the Then clause would be ignored, as it should be.

Finally, to illustrate the Not operator, consider the next diagram, assuming yr = 85 and cent = 1900.

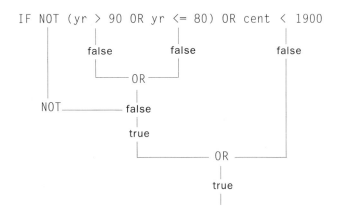

```
IF NOT (yr > 90 OR yr <= 80) OR cent < 1900
```

GUIDED ACTIVITY 5.3

Using Logical Operators

New features of Visual Basic contained in this activity:

- UCase$ function

- Not operator

This activity explores the use of logical operators and introduces the string function UCase$.

1. Start Visual Basic.

2. Create the interface shown in Figure 5.4.

FIGURE 5.4
Interface for Guided Activity 5.3

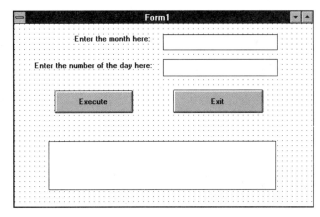

3. Enter an End statement in the Click event for the Exit button.

4. Enter the following code for the Click event of the Execute button.

```
Sub cmdExecute_Click ()
    Picture1.Cls
    MonthYr = txtMonth.Text
    DayNum = txtDay.Text
    If MonthYr = "April" And DayNum = 15 Then
        Picture1.Print "Taxes are due!"
    Else
        Picture1.Print "Taxes are not due."
    End If
    txtMonth.Text = ""
    txtMonth.SetFocus
End Sub
```

CHECKPOINT 5C When is a compound condition statement using And true?

5. Set the Name property for each of the text boxes according to the names shown in the above code.

6. Which clause will be executed if you enter June for the month and 15 for number of the day?

   Try a run and see.

7. Which clause will be executed if you enter April for the month and 15 for number of the day?

   Try a run and see.

8. Enter april (lowercase "a") in the month box.

9. Click Execute. Why does it print that taxes are not due? The reason is that in the If statement, "April" starts with a capital "A." Therefore, for the condition to be true, the user must type the month *exactly* the same as in the If statement.

10. Stop the run.

11. There is a way to fix it so that the computer will accept the month as typed, regardless of what letters are capitalized by the user. We convert them to all capitals with the **UCase$ function**. Change April in the If statement to APRIL. The easy way to do this is to highlight pril with the mouse and type PRIL. The lowercase pril is automatically deleted.

12. In a similar manner, change MonthYr = txtMonth.Text, to MonthYr = UCase$(txtMonth.Text).

13. Start a run and enter april (all lowercase letters) for the month and 15 for the day number. The UCase$ function converts a string into a string with all capital letters.

14. Click Execute.

15. Change And to Or in the If statement and repeat steps 6 and 7.

16. Change the caption on Label1 to `Enter AM or PM:`

17. Change the caption on Label2 to `Enter the time of day (0 to 24):`

18. Change the If/Then/Else statement to the following.

```
If MonthYr = "PM" Or DayNum > 12 Then
        Picture1.Print "It is afternoon"
Else
        Picture1.Print "It is morning"
End If
```

19. Which clause will be executed if you enter AM in the first box and 12 for the time of day? Try a run and see.

20. Which clause will be executed if you enter AM in the first box and 22 for the time of day? Try a run and see.

21. Change the If statement to

```
If Not(MonthYr = "PM") Or DayNum < 12 Then
```

22. Which clause will be executed if you enter AM in the first box and 22 for the time of day? Try it and see.

23. Which clause will be executed if you enter PM in the first box and 10 for the time of day? Try it and see.

24. Change the caption on Label1 to `Enter year:`

25. Change the caption on Label2 to `Enter century:`

26. Change the If/Then/Else statement to the following.

```
If (MonthYr < 90 And MonthYr >= 80) Or DayNum < 1900 Then
    Picture1.Print "The year is in the 80's or it is not the 20th ⏎
        century (or both)"
Else
    Picture1.Print "The year is not in the 80's and it is the 20th ⏎
        century"
End If
```

27. Run the program 4 times, entering the following four pairs for the year and century. In each case, try to predict which clause will be executed before clicking the Execute button.

   a. year = 79, century = 1900

   b. year = 79, century = 1800

   c. year = 85, century = 1900

   d. year = 85, century = 1950

28. Put the word `Not` in front of (MonthYr < 90 And MonthYr >= 80) in the If statement.

CHECKPOINT 5D   What does the Not operator do to a statement?

29.   Repeat step 27. Would you say the statements are equivalent?

30.   Exit Visual Basic without saving anything.

About the New Feature in Guided Activity 5.3

The UCase$ function converts a string argument to all uppercase letters. Only lowercase letters are converted. All other characters in the string remain unchanged.

The UCase$ Function—Syntax

UCase$(*string*)

If you should want to convert a string to all lowercase letters, then use the lowercase counterpart to UCase$, called LCase$. The *LCase$ function* converts a string argument to all lowercase letters. Only uppercase characters in the string are converted, while all other characters in the string remain unchanged.

The LCase$ Function—Syntax

LCase$(*string*)

The Int Function and the Mod Operator

The *greatest integer function,* or Int, is a built-in function with many useful applications. The *Mod operator* returns the value of the remainder of a division operation such as one integer divided by another. We will make use of both in our discussion of the multioption decision structure.

The Int Function

The purpose of Int is to find the largest integer less than an argument x. To illustrate, the value of Int(8.89) is 8, and the value of Int(-2.05) is -3. If x is *positive*, Int(x) simply drops the fractional part of x or *truncates* x to its *integer part*. If x is *negative*, Int(x) equals the nearest integer less than x.

The following table lists a few more examples.

x	$Int(x)$
–2.7	-3
–.35	-1
0	0
.5	0
2.7	2
3.456	3

Another way to remember how Int(x) is evaluated is to realize that every number lies between some integer n and n+1, and that Int(x) equals n.

Rounding Off

To illustrate just one of many applications of this function, we show how it can be used to *round off* a variable called Interest to the nearest cent.

```
Interest = Int(Interest * 100 + .5) / 100
```

The execution of this line for Interest = 40.625 proceeds as follows.

```
Interest = 40.625
Interest * 100 = 4062.5
Interest * 100 + .5 = 4063.0
Int(Interest * 100 + .5) = Int(4063.0) = 4063
Int(Interest * 100 + .5) / 100 = 40.63
```

Thus, after execution the Interest is rounded up to 40.63.

NOTE *In this example the argument is actually a mathematical expression that calls for two calculations before the function Int can be evaluated.*

The Int function can be used to round off a number to any number of decimal places. To round off a number N to three places, use

```
N = Int(N * 1000 + .5) / 1000
```

In general, to round off N to D decimal places, use the formula

```
N = Int(N * 10 ^ D + .5) / 10 ^ D
```

In this formula, 10 ^ D means "10 raised to the power D." For example, to round 5.24137 to the nearest ten-thousandth, let D = 4.

The Mod Operator

To introduce the Mod operator, we consider the problem of determining on which day of the week a given date occurs. A formula to produce the day of the week corresponding to a given date involves the use of the Mod operator and Int. Let N be an integer. When N is divided by a positive integer M, the *remainder* must be one of the numbers 0, 1, ..., M – 1. For instance, if N = 43 and M = 7, then the remainder is 1 since 43 divided by 7 leaves a remainder of 1 or 43 = 6 * 7 + 1.

Mathematically, the remainder is denoted as N Mod M, which is read N modulo M. Thus,

1 = 43 Mod 7
3 = 13 Mod 5 since 13 = 5 * 2 + 3
0 = 52 Mod 13 since 52 = 13 * 4
6 = 231 Mod 9 since 231 = 25 * 9 + 6

In Visual Basic, this remainder can be found using the Mod operator. For example, the statement

```
Print 52 Mod 13
```

will output 0 on the display screen. In general, the statement N Mod M provides the integer value of the remainder of the division of N by M. It can be used in an assignment statement such as

```
Let Remainder = 231 Mod 9
```

When executed, Remainder gets the value of 6.

GUIDED ACTIVITY 5.4

Using Greatest Integer Function Int and the Mod Operator

New features of Visual Basic contained in this activity:

- Integer division

- Int function

- Mod operator

This activity will give you some experience using the Int function and the Mod operator.

1. Start Visual Basic.

2. Create the interface shown in Figure 5.5.

3. Enter an End statement in the Click event for the Exit button.

4. Enter the following code for the Click event of the Execute button.

```
Sub cmdExecute_Click ()
    Picture1.Cls
    x = txtWhlNum.Text
    If Int(x / 2) <> x / 2 Then
        Picture1.Print "The number you entered is odd"
    Else
        Picture1.Print "The number you entered is even"
    End If
    txtWhlNum.Text = ""
    txtWhlNum.SetFocus
End Sub
```

5. Name the text box txtWhlNum.

6. Start a run and enter 12 in the text box, and then click Execute.

   Output:

```
The number you entered is even.
```

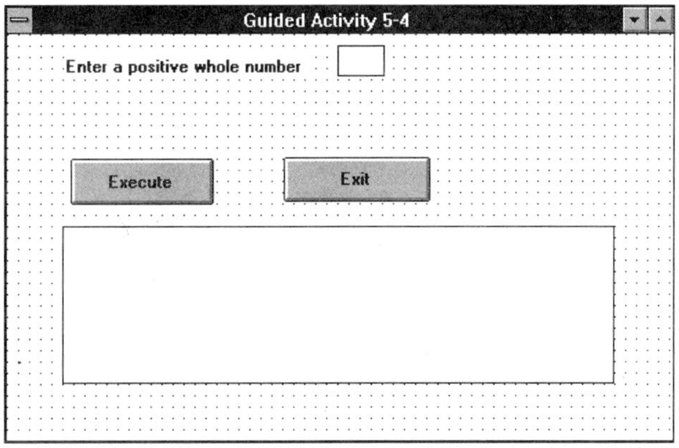

FIGURE 5.5
*User interface
for Guided
Activity 5.4*

7. What would be the output if you enter 13? Try it and see.

8. Add another label to the form below the first label.

9. Change the caption to `Enter another positive whole number less than the first`.

10. Draw a text box next to the new label (about the same size as the first one).

11. Set the Text property of the box to blank.

12. Name the box `txtDivisor`.

13. Add the following line as the third line of cmdExecute_Click.

    ```
    d = txtDivisor.Text
    ```

14. Given two positive whole numbers x and d, d < x, then x = (*Quotient*) * d + *Remainder*. It follows that the *Remainder* = x - (*Quotient*) * d. To illustrate, add the following lines to the same procedure immediately following the End If statement.

    ```
    Picture1.Print "The quotient is "; Int(x / d)
    Picture1.Print "The remainder is "; x - Int(x / d) * d
    ```

15. Start a run and enter 25 for first number and 6 for the second, and then click Execute.

    Output:

    ```
    The quotient is 4
    The remainder is 1
    ```

16. There is another type of division, called ***integer division***. This operation truncates the quotient of division to an integer. It is denoted by the *backslash* (\) in contrast to the forward slash (/), which indicates ordinary division. To see the result of the backslash, enter the following line in the cmdExecute procedure following the other Print statements.

    ```
    Picture1.Print 10 \ 4, 24.5 \ 3, -24.5 \ 5, 35.9 \ 6.2, 35.9 \ -6.2
    ```

17. Start a run and enter 10 and 4 in the text boxes and click Execute.

Output:

```
The number you entered is even
The quotient is 2
The remainder is 2
2    8    -4    6    -6        .
```

18. Integer division can be used to produce the same result as the Mod operator. Add the following line to the cmdExecute procedure following the line addition made in step 16.

```
Picture1.Print x; "\"; d; "equals "; Int(x/d)
y = x \ d
Remainder = x - d * y
Picture1.Print "The remainder = "; Remainder, x; "Mod "; ⤶
     d " = "; x Mod d
```

19. Start a run and enter 27 and 4 in the text boxes and click Execute.

Output:

```
The number you entered is odd
The quotient is 6
The remainder is 3
2    8    -4    6    -6
27 \ 4 equals 6
The remainder is 3    27 Mod 4 = 3
```

20. The Mod operator can be used to test if a number is even or odd. Add the following line at the end of the list of Print lines.

```
Picture1.Print x Mod 2, d Mod 2
```

21. Start a run and enter 36 and 35, respectively, and click Execute.

NOTE *A number is even if the remainder when divided by 2 is 0 and odd when the remainder is 1.*

22. Exit Visual Basic without saving (unless you want to).

To see how the Mod operator can be used to solve the problem of finding what day of the week a given date will fall on, let DayWeek denote the day of the week on which a given date occurs. We use 0 for Saturday, 1 for Sunday, 2 for Monday, and so on. The value of DayWeek is determined by first finding the value of DWeek Mod 7 where

```
DWeek = 2 + Dmon + 2 * NMonth + Int(.61 * (NMonth + 1)) + TYear
```

and

```
TYear = Yr + Int(Yr / 4) - Int(Yr / 100) + Int(Yr / 400).
```

The other variables are as follows:

NMonth = Number of the month
Dmon = Number of day of the month
Yr = Any year after 1582.

For the above formula to work properly, some adjustment is required for the month and year. The month of January is treated as the *thirteenth* month and February as the *fourteenth* month of the *previous* year. For example, 2/13/1994 must be changed to 14/13/1993.

For an illustration, suppose we want the day of the week for February 13, 1994. In this case, NMonth = 14 and Dmon = 13 and Yr = 1993 (after making the adjustments outlined above) then

$$TYear = 1993 + Int(1993 / 4) - Int(1993 / 100) + Int(1993 / 400)$$
$$= 1993 + 498 - 19 + 4$$
$$= 2476$$

$$DWeek = 2 + 13 + 2*14 + Int(.61 * 15) + 2476$$
$$= 2 + 13 + 28 + 9 + 2476$$
$$= 2528$$

Finally, DayWeek = 2528 Mod 7 = 1, which makes February 13, 1994, fall on a Sunday.

Here is the *first part* of a procedure to determine what day of the week a given date falls on, using ideas presented so far.

```
Sub cmdDayWeek_Click ()
Rem Variable List:
Rem   NMonth = Number of month
Rem   Dmon = Number of the day of the month
Rem   Yr = Any year after 1582
Rem   TYear = Temporary value for year calculation
Rem   DWeek = Dividend used by Mod operator to find DayWeek
Rem   DayWeek = Number of day of week (Sat = 0, Sun = 1, Etc.)
Rem ****************************************************************
Rem Adjust for month and year
      NMonth = txtMonth.Text: Dmon = txtDmon.Text: Yr = txtYear.Text
      If NMonth = 1 Or NMonth = 2 Then
          NMonth = NMonth + 12
          Yr = Yr - 1
      End If
Rem Compute DWeek and DayWeek
      DWeek = 2 | Dmon + 2 * NMonth + Int(.61 * (NMonth + 1))
      TYear = Yr + Int(Yr / 4) - Int(Yr / 100) + Int(Yr / 400)
      DWeek = DWeek + TYear
      DayWeek = DWeek Mod 7
      Picture1.Cls
End Sub
```

The Multioption Block Select Case Statement

To *finish* our procedure we started above, we show how to have the computer print the day of the week corresponding to the given date. What day it is depends on the variable DayWeek. If DayWeek is 0 (zero), then the computer should print that the date entered falls on a Saturday. If it is a 1, then it should output the day as a Sunday and so on. This type of alternative action on the part of the computer is handled very well using a multioption decision structure called Select Case.

The Select Case Statement—Syntax

```
Select Case testexpression
Case expression list # 1
[statement block # 1]
[Case expression list # 2]
[statement block # 2]
        .
        .
        .
[Case Else]
[statement block to be executed if none of the other Case statement blocks is executed]
End Select
```

Block Structure

The Select Case statement is another example of a **block structure**; it starts with the key words Select Case and terminates with End Select. In between these key words is a list of cases, each consisting of a block of one or more statements to be executed according to the value of the test expression. Whichever case the value of the test expression corresponds to is the block of statements that is executed.

A diamond is the flowchart symbol used with the Select Case statement to show that a decision is required by the computer as to what statement will be executed next, as shown in Figure 5.6.

The flowchart indicates that the computer follows the YES path out of the decision diamond if the value of the test expression agrees with one of the expressions in the corresponding Case expression list; otherwise, it follows the NO path. The statements in the Else block are executed when the test value fails to agree with any of the Case lists.

In the case of our current program, the flowchart is shown in Figure 5.7.

Following this flowchart, we finish our procedure with the following code.

```
Select Case DayWeek
      Case 0
      Picture1.Print "The date entered falls on a Saturday"
      Case 1
      Picture1.Print "The date entered falls on a Sunday"
      Case 2
```

```
Picture1.Print "The date entered falls on a Monday"
Case 3
Picture1.Print "The date entered falls on a Tuesday"
Case 4
Picture1.Print "The date entered falls on a Wednesday"
Case 5
```

FIGURE 5.6
A flowchart for the Select Case statement

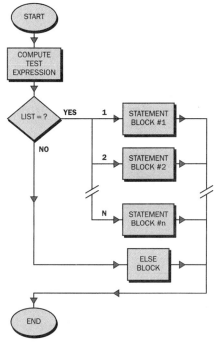

FIGURE 5.7
A flowchart for the Select Case statement of cmdDayWeek

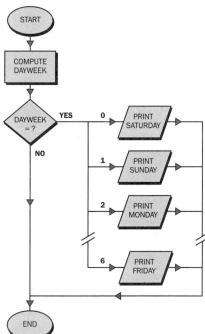

```
            Picture1.Print "The date entered falls on a Thursday"
            Case 6
            Picture1.Print "The date entered falls on a Friday"
    End Select
    End Sub
```

This statement works in the following manner. After the first part of the procedure determines the value of DayWeek, which must be an integer between 0 and 6, the Select Case statement branches to the correct print statement according to its value. For example, if DayWeek = 6, then Select Case jumps to Case 6 and prints `The date entered falls on a Friday` and then proceeds to the End Select statement.

Here is the finished procedure.

Day of the Week Procedure

```
    Sub cmdDayWeek_Click ()
    Rem Variable List:
    Rem   NMonth = Number of month
    Rem   Dmon = Number of the day of the month
    Rem   Year = Any year after 1582
    Rem   TYear = Temporary value for year calculation
    Rem   DWeek = Dividend used by Mod operator to find DayWeek
    Rem   DayWeek = Number of day of week (Sat = 0, Sun = 1, Etc.)
    Rem   ***********************************************************
    Rem Adjust for month and year
          NMonth = txtMonth.Text: Dmon = txtDmon.Text: Yr = txtYear.Text
          If NMonth = 1 Or NMonth = 2 Then
              NMonth = NMonth + 12
              Yr = Yr - 1
          End If
    Rem Compute DWeek and DayWeek
          DWeek = 2 + Dmon + 2 * NMonth + Int(.61 * (NMonth + 1))
          TYear = Yr + Int(Yr / 4) - Int(Yr / 100) + Int(Yr / 400)
          DWeek = DWeek + TYear
          DayWeek = DWeek Mod 7
          Picture1.Cls
    Select Case DayWeek
          Case 0
          Picture1.Print "The date entered falls on a Saturday"
          Case 1
          Picture1.Print "The date entered falls on a Sunday"
          Case 2
          Picture1.Print "The date entered falls on a Monday"
          Case 3
          Picture1.Print "The date entered falls on a Tuesday"
          Case 4
```

```
          Picture1.Print "The date entered falls on a Wednesday"
          Case 5
          Picture1.Print "The date entered falls on a Thursday"
          Case 6
          Picture1.Print "The date entered falls on a Friday"
     End Select
     End Sub
```

GUIDED ACTIVITY 5.5

Using the Select Case Statement

New feature of Visual Basic contained in this activity:

- Select Case statement

  This activity illustrates the Select Case statement through the Day of the Week Application.

1. Start Visual Basic.

2. Draw the interface shown in Figure 5.8.

FIGURE 5.8
*Interface for the
Day of Week
Application*

3. Enter an End statement into the Click event for the Exit button.

4. Name the three text boxes txtMonth, txtDmon, and txtYear, respectively.

5. Enter the code for the cmdDayWeek_Click procedure.

6. Start a run and enter 2 for the month, 13 for the day of the month, and 1994 for the year.

7. Click the Day of Week button. The given day falls on a Sunday.

8. Highlight the 2 in the month box with the mouse and type 9.

9. Highlight the 13 in the day box and type 14.

10. Highlight the year in the year box and type 1995.

11. Click the Day of Week button. The output should be that the given date falls on a Thursday.

12. Get a calendar and try some other dates of your own choosing.

13. Save as dayweek.

14. Exit Visual Basic.

Keyword Syntax Review

Keyword—Syntax	Purpose
And	To create a compound conditional statement
End If	To mark the end of a block If/Then statement.
End Select	To mark the end of a block Select Case statement
Exit Sub	To immediately exit from a procedure

If (*condition*) Then
    [*statement block*]
End If
	To construct a single option decision structure

If (*condition*) Then
    [*statement block*]
Else
    [*statement block*]
End If
	To construct a dual option decision structure

Int(*argument*)	To find the integer part of the *argument*
LCase$(*string*)	To convert all letter characters in *string* to lowercase
n Mod m	To find the remainder when integer n is divided by m
Not	To negate a logical statement

Select Case *testexpression*
    Case *expression list # 1*
        [*statement block # 1*]
    [Case *expression list # 2*]
        [*statement block # 2*]
    .
    .
    .
    [Case Else]
        [*statement block*]
End Select
	To construct a multioption decision structure

UCase$(*string*)	To convert all letter characters in *string* to uppercase

EXERCISE 5.1

Bank Statement Data

Write a procedure that will read a series of bank transactions from a file and print the following information.

1. Total number of checks.

2. Total amount of checks.

3. Total number of deposits.

4. Total amount deposited.

Test data:

150, -23.95, -50, -12.95, 450, 321, -75.99, -89, 254.55, -103.56, 156.79

A *positive* number means the transaction was a *deposit*. A *negative* number means the transaction was a *check*. The test data contains 6 checks and 5 deposits.

EXERCISE 5.2

Property Tax

Write an application to print a two-column table giving the value of the property and the tax. Compute and print the total property value and the total tax at the bottom of each column. The taxes are computed according to the following table.

Value	Tax
$0–49,999	$500.00
$50,000–75,999	$500 + 1.5% of value
$75,000–99,999	$700 + 2% of value
$100,000–250,000	$800 + 2.5% of value
Over $250,000	2% of value

Use the logical operators and If/Then/Else statement to decide how the tax is computed. Test your program with the following property values: $300,000, $140,000, $89,000, $65,300, and $32,000.

Output:

```
        Value          Tax
        $300,000.00    $6,000.00
        $140,000.00    $4,300.00
        $89,000.00     $2,480.00
        $65,300.00     $1,479.50
        $32,000.00     $500.00
Totals  $626,300.00    $14,759.50
```

EXERCISE 5.3

Data Search

1. Write an application to count how many club members are over 21. Have the computer read the names and ages from a file.

   Output:

   ```
   The number of members over 21 is 7
   ```

2. Modify your procedure to count how many are teenagers and how many are over 50. Have the program print a list of names of those over 50.

   Output:

   ```
   The number of teenagers is 2
   The following members are over 50: Adams, Hale, Lyle
   ```

   Test Data: Name, Age

   Adams, 52, Bates, 18, Collins, 21, Doaks, 42, Evans, 32, Fox, 16, Hale, 65, Jones, 35, Kates, 22, Lyle, 56

EXERCISE 5.4

Allowable Charge Limit Check

Write an application to print a list of charge account numbers that have exceeded their credit limit. A file contains the account number, the beginning balance, the total charges for the month, and the credit limit. Your program must compute the new balance, compare it to the limit, and report if it is over the limit. If

(Beginning Balance + Total Charges for the Month) > Limit

then the account has exceeded its limit.

Output:

```
The following accounts have exceeded their credit limit:
A411, T341
```

Test Data:

Acc. #	Beginning Bal.	Total Charges	Limit
A215	598.16	126.10	4000
A411	2998.00	46.50	3000
C981	1500.00	498.00	2000
R253	783.46	126.50	1000
T341	3461.10	625.15	4000

EXERCISE 5.5

Credit Card Service Charge

A credit card company charges a monthly service charge of 1.5% on the first $750.00 of the balance and 1% on the amount of the balance above $750.00. Thus, if *Balance* <= 750, the *Service Charge* = 0.065 * *Balance,* and if *Balance* > 750, the *Service Charge* = 0.015 * 750 + 0.01 * (*Balance* - 750). Write an application to print the account number and the service charge.

Test Data:

Acc. #	Balance
T106	1500.00
S451	356.00
S452	750.00
AB56	751.00
R201	1198.91

EXERCISE 5.6

Registered Voter Information

Write an application to read statistical data on a group of voters from a file and print a list of the Democrats who are married and have incomes of *at least* $50,000.00. Read the name, party affiliation, and marital status as strings. Use the logical operators to select the proper names for the list.

Test Data:

Name	Party	Income	Marital Status
Adams	Rep.	250,000	Single
Brock	Ind.	70,000	Married
Cates	Rep	75,000	Single
Doaks	Dem.	150,000	Married
Davids	Dem.	50,001	Married
Fuchs	Rep.	25,000	Single
Hill	Ind.	15,500	Single
Jones	Dem	55,000	Married
Rich	Dem.	49,000	Married
Smith	Dem	100,000	Single

EXERCISE 5.7

School Class Level

Using the Select Case statement, write an application to print a list showing the name and the class for a group of students. The program should print `Freshman`, `Sophomore`, `Junior`, or `Senior`, according to the class level number 1, 2, 3, or 4, respectively.

Test Data: Name, Class Level

Adams, 2, Bates, 1, Cates, 3, Doaks, 1, Doe, 4, Lake, 3, Monk, 2, Peters, 4, Rich, 2, Smith, 3

EXERCISE 5.8

Cost of Pizza

Rudy's Pizza Palace serves three sizes of pizza—small, medium, and large. The small pizza sells for $5.50, the medium for $6.75, and the large for $9.50. Using the Select Case statement, write an application to print the cost of a pizza according to a selection number entered by the user.

Review Questions

*1. When is the following relational expression true?

```
Int(Value / 2) <> Value / 2
```

2. In the following procedure X = -2 and Y = -3. After the If/Then statement, which line is executed next? What value is printed?

```
Sub Command1.Click()
If X > Y Then
      X = X + 2
Else
      Y = Y + 3
End If
Print X + Y
End Sub
```

*3. Identify what is wrong, if anything, with the following segment of code. If there is something wrong, how would you correct it?

```
X = Text1.Text
If Int(X / 2) = X / 2 Then
      Print "X IS ODD"
Else
      Print "X IS EVEN"
End If
```

*4. Identify the errors, if any, in the following lines. Consider each line separately. Give suggestions for ways to correct the errors.

a.
```
If X * Y Then
    A = 27
End If
```

b.
```
If t + 1 > 2, Then
    Comm = 57
End If
```

c.
```
If -10 < X < 20 Then
    T = T + 1
End If
```

d.
```
If (Mer$ = "PM" Or Hr > 12) Then
    Print "It is afternoon"
Else
    Print "It is morning"
End If
```

*5. Determine the purpose of the following segment of code and fill in the blank. Describe how it works.

```
A = Text1.Text: B = Text2.Text
If A < B Then
    A = B
End If
Print "The _____ number is ", A
```

6. Rewrite the following block If/Then/Else so that it will accomplish exactly the same task using the *negation* of the condition given.

```
If Rate <= .06 Then
    COMM = Rate * Price + 500
Else
    COMM = Rate * (Price - Discount) + 750
End If
```

*7. Write a block If/Then/Else statement that will determine and print if a given number is positive, negative, or zero.

8. Explain for which values of X the Then block will be executed and for which the Else block will be executed.

```
If Int(X / 3) <> (X / 3) Then
    Print "This is the Then block"
Else
    Print "This is the Else block"
End If
```

9. Give an application for the Mod operator.

10. What is the truth value of (50 < 75 Or 90 > 100) And 110 = 120?

*11. What is the truth value of 50 < 75 Or (90 > 100 And 110 = 120)?

12. What is the value of Int(X) for a number X?

*13. What is the value of - Int(-3.2)?

14. Explain in detail the execution of Int(X * 100 + .5) / 100 for X = 75.856.

15. Write a line that will round off a number X to four decimal places.

*16. What does X = Int(X + .5) do to a positive X?

17. Evaluate each of the following:

    a. Int(3.4)

    b. Int(-9.8)

    c. Int(45)

    d. Int(34.678) / 100

    e. Int(0)

    f. Int(.75)

    g. Int(3 * 4)

    h. Int(3 * 4.1 + 2.8)

    i. Int(34.678 + .5) / 100

    j. Int(-.5)

*18. What is the function of the Select Case statement?

Important Terms

Block structure	Integer part	Round off
Decision structure	LCase$ function	Single
Dual option decision structure	Mod operator	Single option decision structure
Floating point	Multioption decision structure	Truncate
Frame	Option button	UCase$ function
Greatest integer function	Real	Unary operator
Integer division	Remainder	Value property

Data Structures

The simple variables used in the previous units were our first examples of data structures. In this unit we introduce more complex data structures known as arrays that provide new ways for a program to store and manipulate data. The applications will include sorting and alphabetization.

Learning Objectives

At the completion of this unit you should know

1. how to define a data structure called an array,

2. how to dimension an array,

3. what a subscript is,

4. how to create general procedures and subroutines,

5. how to sort a list of numbers,

6. how to alphabetize,

7. how to use the MsgBox function,

8. how to use the Printer object,

9. how to use the EndDoc method,

10. how to use list boxes and combo boxes.

Important Keywords

AddItem

Call

Dim

EndDoc

GoSub

Printer

ReDim

RemoveItem

Return

Subscripted Variables

Our method of naming variables has been adequate up to this point. However, in the Payroll Application, each time a new employee's name is read, the old name is lost. The same is true of the hours and the rates.

Suppose we want to retain each employee's name for use elsewhere in the program. For example, we may want to print an alphabetized list of employees, compute the average hourly rate, or compute the average number of hours worked. Since there are six employees, we would need six different variable names to hold the names, six for hours, and six for the rates. We could do this, but how would we conveniently change the names within the loop in cmdPayRol? What if there were 100 employees?

Fortunately, Visual Basic provides us with another method of creating variable names by means of an *index* or *subscript*. Using subscripts, a series of distinct variable names forming a *data structure* called an *array* can be defined. In standard mathematical notation, a subscript is attached to the bottom of a letter. For example, A_1, A_2, N_3, and M_{15} are subscripted variables read as "A sub one," "A sub two," "N sub three," and "M sub fifteen," respectively.

In Visual Basic, these same variables are denoted as A(1), A(2), N(3), and M(15), respectively. The parentheses are *actually part of* the name, distinguishing them from A1, A2, N3, and M15.

Since the subscript is variable, we can change a subscripted variable's name by simply changing the subscript value. A variable name such as A(I) (read "A sub I") denotes the Ith element of a *one-dimensional array* of variables, one variable for each value of I. For I = 1, we have variable A(1), for I = 2 we have variable A(2), and so on. If I varies from 1 to 10, then A(I) stands for any one of the ten variables A(1), A(2), ..., A(10) depending on the value of I. In terms of memory cells, there are ten memory cells associated with A(I) where I is the cell number. The subscript I is also

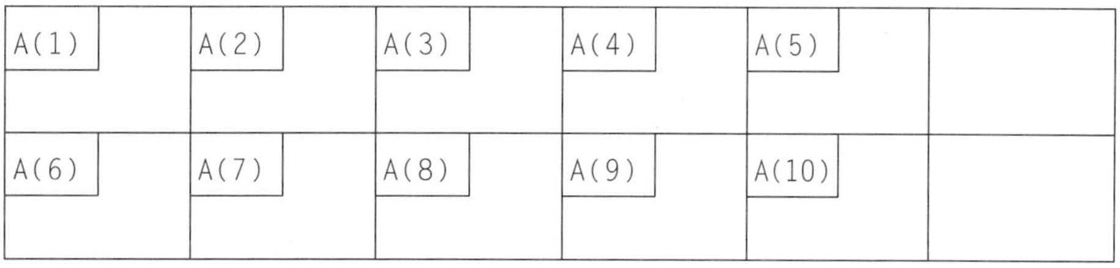

FIGURE 6.1
Memory cells for an array

| A(1) | A(2) | A(3) | A(4) | A(5) | |
| A(6) | A(7) | A(8) | A(9) | A(10) | |

called a *pointer* since it points to a certain array cell, as shown in Figure 6.1. Similarly, we can use subscripts with string variables as well.

To illustrate, let's modify the cmdPayRol procedure to retain each employee's name, the hours worked, and the hourly rate using subscripted variables. The changes are in boldface.

```
Sub cmdPayRol_Click ()
' Initialize employee counter and the total payroll accumulator
Empl = 0
Total = 0
Picture1.Print "Employee"; Tab(15); "Hours"; Tab(26); "Rate"; Tab(35); ↵
    "Gross Pay"
Do Until EOF(1)
    Empl = Empl + 1
    Input #1, EmplName(Empl), Hours(Empl), HrRate(Empl)
    Wages(Empl) = Hours(Empl) * HrRate(Empl)
    Total = Total + Wages(Empl)
    Picture1.Print Tab(2); EmplName(Empl); Tab(15); Hours(Empl); ↵
        Tab(25); HrRate(Empl); Tab(35); Format$(Wages(Empl), "currency")
    Picture1.Print
Loop
Picture1.Print "The Total Payroll for the Week is "; Format$(Total, ↵
    "currency")
End Sub
```

Dimensioning an Array

We declare all of the arrays as module-level variables using two Dim statements placed in the (general) object of the form. The (general) object is also referred to as the ***Declarations section*** of the code module. These arrays are called ***static arrays*** since their size is set *at design time* and cannot be resized.

```
Dim EmplName(6) As String
Dim Hours(6), HrRate(6), Wages(6)
```

The Dim Statement for Arrays—Syntax

Dim *array name* (*largest subscript*) As *type*

or

Dim *array name* (*smallest subscript* To *largest subscript*) As *type*

The *array name* follows the same rules as for naming variables. The *smallest subscript* and the *largest subscript* are integers between -32,768 and 32,767, inclusive, indicating the range of the subscripts. A subscript may be any number within that range, including zero, or a numeric expression. In the first case, zero is the lowest subscript by default. If a subscript is not a whole number, it is rounded to the nearest whole number.

The clause As *type* is used to declare the data type of the array. This may be any of the types we have seen so far (Integer, Single, String, Variant) or one of several others mentioned below. All members of the array are of the same type. The Dim statement automatically initializes all members of a numerical array to zero and all members of a Variant or string array to null strings.

Examples

The following allocates 56 cells for Variant data and 56 cells for string data.

```
Dim Score(55), FName(55) As String
```

All 56 elements of both arrays are filled with blanks.

This next example allocates arrays for 21 floating-point values and 21 integers.

```
Dim Taxes(20) As Single, Empl(20) As Integer
```

Table 6.1 is a list of the available data types.

TYPE	DESCRIPTION	DECLARATION CHARACTER
Currency	8-byte number with two decimal places	@
Double	8-byte floating point	#
Integer	2-byte integer	%
Long	4-byte integer	&
Single	4-byte floating point	!
String	String of characters	$
Variant	Date/time, floating point number, or string	(None)

TABLE 6.1 *Fundamental data types*

The declaration character can be used to declare a variable type by attaching it to the variable name. For example, the statement

```
Dim FName$, Taxes!(20), Empl%(20)
```

declares the variable FName as a string variable, Taxes as an array of floating point numbers of type Single, and Empl as an array of integers.

NOTE *Visual Basic allows more than one way to declare a variable. For example, Empl%(20) is equivalent to Dim Empl(20) As Integer.*

GUIDED ACTIVITY 6.1

Exploring the Dim Statement and Subscripted Variables

New features of Visual Basic contained in this activity:

- Declaration characters

  This activity gives some details concerning the Dim statement and subscripted variables.

1. Start Visual Basic.

2. Draw two command buttons and a picture box on the form.

3. Enter the captions Execute and Exit on these buttons.

4. Name one button cmdExecute and the other cmdExit.

5. Enter an End statement in cmdExit_Click.

6. Enter the following Dim statement in the (general) object.

   ```
   Dim Member%(12), Element$(12)
   ```

7. Enter the following procedure in cmdExecute_Click to show that Visual Basic automatically initializes all values of a numeric array to zero and a string array to blanks.

   ```
   For K = 0 To 12
        Picture1.Print Member%(K); Element$(K)
   Next K
   ```

8. Run this procedure and look carefully at the output. It shows the initial values of the two arrays.

   Partial Output:

   ```
   0
   0
   0
   Etc.
   ```

9. Open Notepad and create a file containing the following two lines. Save the file as ga6-1.dat.

   ```
   A, B, C, D, E, F, G, H, I, J, K, L, M
   100, 101, 102, 103, 104, 105, 106, 107, 108, 109, 110, 111, 112
   ```

10. Add the following Open statement in the Form_Load procedure.

    ```
    Open "ga6-1.dat" For Input As #1
    ```

11. Add the following lines to the procedure inside the loop just before the print statement.

```
Input #1, Element$(K)
Member(K) = K + 1
```

12. Run the procedure again. The output shows how values are assigned to arrays.

    Partial Output:

```
1 A
2 B
3 C
4 D
Etc.
```

13. Delete the For/Next loop in cmdExecute.

14. Change the Dim statement in the (general) object to:

```
Dim Member%(10 To 22), Element$(10 To 22)
```

15. Add the following two loops to cmdExecute.

```
For i = 0 To 12
    Input #1, Element(I + 10)
Next i
For i = 0 To 12
    Input #1, Member(I + 10)
Next i
```

16. Enter the following loop in cmdExecute below those of step 15.

```
For J = 10 To 22
    Picture1.Print Member(J); "   "; Element(J)
Next J
```

17. Run this procedure and observe the output. Notice the two different ways subscripts are handled in this segment.

    Output:

```
100    A
101    B
102    C
  .
  .
112    M
```

    This output shows that the subscript can be an expression and that it must be a number between 10 and 22.

18. Exit Visual Basic without saving.

Sorting by Selection

To further illustrate the use of subscripted variables, let's consider the problem of sorting an array of numbers from the smallest number to the largest.

The first step is to decide on a method of sorting numbers that can be computerized. To find a method, we begin with a question: How would we sort these numbers by hand with pencil and paper? One way would be to simply look at the list of numbers, pick out the smallest, and make it the first. Then look at the remaining numbers, pick out the smallest, and make it the second in the list, and so on.

This sorting method rests on two fundamental steps:

- Find the smallest number in the list.

- Exchange it with the first number in the list.

The process begins by applying these two steps to the entire list of N numbers. The steps are then repeated on the remaining N-1 numbers, then on the remaining N-2 numbers, and so on until there is only one number left, which must be the largest.

To make it easier to program, let's try it by hand for the following 10 numbers.

```
503 61 127 908 154 677 523 87 897 500
```

The first step is to find the smallest number among these 10 numbers. Letting X stand for the smallest number, we begin by setting X = A(1) = 503, and compare it with each of the remaining numbers. If we find a smaller number in the list, we set X equal to this new number and record its subscript. Starting with X = 503, we compare it with A(2) = 61, which is smaller. We set X = 61, store the subscript (2) as K, and then continue comparing with the rest of the list. No smaller number will be found; therefore, we exchange A(1) = 503 with A(K) = A(2) = 61. This exchange is necessary for two reasons: (1) to put the smallest number at the beginning of this list and (2) to retain the number that was at the beginning. This yields

```
61 503 127 908 154 677 523 87 897 500
```

61 is now in the proper place and we move on to the second position and repeat the process.

This time, we start with X = A(2) = 503. Comparing 503 with A(3) = 127, we see that 127 is smaller. Thus, we set X = A(3) = 127, K = 3, and continue. Now, we compare the remaining numbers with 127. No smaller number is found until we reach A(8) = 87. At this point, X is set equal to 87 and K to 8. The last two numbers are larger; hence, we exchange A(2) with A(K) = A(8) to obtain

```
61 87 127 908 154 677 523 503 897 500
```

We now have two numbers in their proper places. The process is repeated for the remaining eight numbers. We continue until the numbers are in order, shown in Figure 6.2.

A procedure to carry out the selection sort requires three parts— one to read the numbers to be sorted, one to do the actual sorting, and one to output the sorted list. We describe the sorting procedure using *pseudocode*. Pseudocode is used to outline a procedure employing very concise statements to describe the various tasks and the

FIGURE 6.2
Summary of the selection method of sorting

ORIGINAL LIST	503	61	127	980	154	677	523	87	897	500
1	61	503	127	908	154	677	523	87	987	500
2	61	87	127	908	154	677	523	503	897	500
3	61	87	127	908	154	677	523	503	897	500
4	61	87	127	154	908	677	523	503	897	500
5	61	87	127	154	500	677	523	503	897	908
6	61	87	127	154	500	503	523	677	897	908
7	61	87	127	154	500	503	523	677	897	908
8	61	87	127	154	500	503	523	677	897	908
9	61	87	127	154	500	503	523	677	897	908

control logic. It uses statements that resemble actual program statements but are written in ordinary English utilizing mathematical symbols and elements of the Visual Basic language. Pseudocode allows the programmer to think freely about a procedure without worrying about syntax details. One way to generate pseudocode is to think of how to perform the tasks by hand and then write a brief set of instructions similar to computer instructions.

We begin with pseudocode for the sorting routine described above.

Pseudocode for SelectionSort Procedure

```
For I = 1 To N-1
      Let X equal the first number in the list A(I) which
      is a candidate for the smallest in the list
      Let K be the subscript of the first number in the list (I)
      Rem Began a comparison of X with the rest of the list
      For J = I + 1 To N
         If A(J) < X Then
         Set X equal to the smaller number A(J) and set K
         equal to its subscript J
      Next J
      Exchange smallest number in list (subscript K) with the
      first number in the list (subscript I)
Next I
```

Using the pseudocode the procedure is coded as follows.

The Code for the SelectionSort Procedure

```
cmdSelectionSort_Click ()
      For I = 1 To n - 1
         X = A(I)
         K = I
```

```
    For J = I + 1 To n
        If A(J) < X Then
            X = A(J)
            K = J
        End If
    Next J
Rem Swap smallest with first number in list
    A(K) = A(I)
    A(I) = X
Next I
End Sub
```

For each list under consideration (that is, A(J) for J = I to n - 1), the variable X stands for the smallest number and K its subscript. The first number in the list could be the smallest; therefore, before each search, the computer sets X = A(I), the first number in the current list, and sets X = I, the subscript of the first number in the list. The computer then proceeds to check each of the remaining numbers against X (see the J-Loop). As long as A(J) remains greater than or equal to X, X remains the same. If an A(J) is found that is smaller, then X is set equal to A(J), and K is set to the subscript J. When the computer exits from the J-Loop, X equals the smallest number in the list, and K is its subscript. The process is completed by exchanging the first number in the current list with the smallest.

Dynamic Arrays

In this example we use a *dynamic array* to store the list of numbers to be sorted. This way we do not need to know ahead of time how many items are in the array. The size of a dynamic array is set *at run time* and can be resized at any time. Otherwise, the usefulness of the procedure would be limited by a *preset* array size. We could preset the size fairly large, but that would be inefficient use of memory. With a dynamic array, we can use the same procedure regardless of the number of elements to be sorted.

To create a dynamic array, we use a Dim statement with an *empty* set of parentheses in the Declarations section if we want it to be module-level and in the procedure itself for a local array (visible to the procedure only). For example,

```
Dim SortList()
```

establishes SortList as a dynamic array.

The allocation of the actual number of array elements is accomplished with a ReDim statement.

The ReDim Statement—Syntax

ReDim *variable name* (*subscripts*) [As *type*]

The *subscripts* and As *type* parts of this statement have the same meaning as they do for the Dim statement.

The ReDim Statement—Examples

```
ReDim SortList(n)
ReDim Roster(15), ClassList(10 to 30)
ReDim Employee(x + 1)
```

A Sorting Application

We begin with the Declarations section of the (general) object. In it we declare a dynamic array to hold the list of numbers and a variable n as the size of the list.

Code for the (general) Object

```
Dim A(), n
```

Next, we use the Form_Load procedure to open the file and to read the value of n from the file, to dimension the array, and to read in the list of numbers.

Code for the Form_Load Procedure

```
Sub Form_Load ()
    Open "selsrt.dat" For Input As #1
    Input #1, n
    ReDim A(n)
    For i = 1 To n
        Input #1, A(i)
    Next i
End Sub
```

The procedure that does the sort and prints the results is called cmdSelSrt.

Code for the cmdSelSrt Procedure

```
Sub cmdSelSrt_Click ()
For I = 1 To n - 1
    X = A(I)
    K = I
    For J = I + 1 To n
        If A(J) < X Then
        X = A(J)
        K = J
        End If
    Next J
    A(K) = A(I)
    A(I) = X
Next I
    Picture1.Cls
    Picture1.Print "Here is the sorted list of numbers"
```

```
        Picture1.Print
        For I = 1 To n
            Picture1.Print A(i);
        Next i
End Sub
```

Code for the cmdExit Procedure

```
Sub cmdExit_Click ()
        Close #1
        End
End Sub
```

Using Notepad, we create a data file called `selsrt.dat` containing the ten numbers we want to sort. The first number in the file is the number of numbers. Here is the single line of data for the file.

```
10, 503, 61, 127, 980, 154, 677, 523, 87, 897, 500
```

GUIDED ACTIVITY 6.2

Testing the Selection Sort

New features of Visual Basic contained in this activity:

- Call statement
- Dynamic array
- General procedures
- ReDim statement

In this activity you'll see how the selection sort puts a list of numbers into either ascending or descending order (the user's choice). Also, you'll explore how to create a new procedure and activate it with a Call statement.

1. Open Notepad and create the file `selsrt.dat`.

2. Save the file in the appropriate directory.

3. Start Visual Basic.

4. Create an interface containing two command buttons captioned as `Sort List` and `Exit` and named `cmdSelSrt` and `cmdExit`, respectively.

5. Add a picture box with dimensions roughly 1 inch high by 5 inches wide.

6. Open the Code window for the Sort List button and enter the code given.

7. Open the Exit button and enter its code.

8. Switch to the (general) object and enter the Dim statement.

CHECKPOINT 6A How do you switch between objects?

9. Switch to the Form object and enter the code for the Form_Load procedure.

10. Start a run and make any adjustments necessary to get a successful run.

11. Click Exit to stop the run.

12. At this point, we plan to make it possible for the user to choose between an ascending sort and a descending sort by means of two option buttons. Draw a frame on the form about 1 inch by 2 inches.

13. Change the caption on the frame to Ascending or Descending?

14. Add an option button to the frame.

15. Change its caption to Ascending and its name to optAscend.

16. Add the second option button to the frame.

17. Change its caption to Descending and its name to optDescend. Figure 6.3 shows the modified interface.

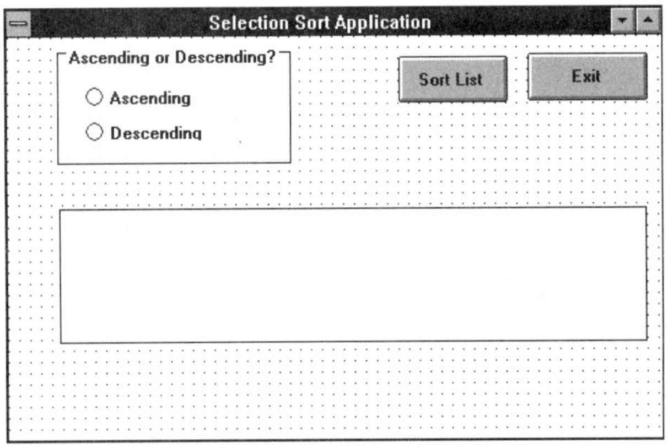

FIGURE 6.3
*Modified
interface
for Guided
Activity 6.2*

18. Open the Code window for cmdSelSrt and highlight the sorting routine.

19. Select Cut from the Edit menu.

20. Next, we introduce *general procedures*. A general procedure is the same as an event procedure, with one exception. It is not tied to an object and, therefore, does not require an event to be activated. Switch to the (general) object.

21. Click the View title on the menu bar and select the New Procedure option or press [Alt][V] and then press [N].

22. Click Sub in the dialog box shown in Figure 6.4 and enter AscendSort in the Name box.

23. Click OK.

FIGURE 6.4
New Procedure
dialog box

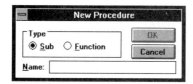

24. Select Paste from the Edit menu. You should now have the sorting routine in your new procedure.

25. Click the arrow on the end of the Proc. box. This new procedure should be listed.

26. Click anywhere in the AscendSort procedure.

27. Repeat steps 21 through 24 using `DescendSort` for the name.

28. To sort the numbers in descending order, we need to change less than (<) to greater than (>) in the sorting routine. Make this change now.

29. Switch back to cmdSelSrt. In place of the sorting routine, enter the following code immediately above the output statements.

```
If optAscend.Value = True Then
     Call AscendSort
Else
     Call DescendSort
End If
```

NOTE *The Call statement transfers control to either AscendSort or DescendSort according to the truth value of optAscend. The Call keyword is optional, but adds clarity when reading code.*

The Call Statement—Syntax

[`Call`] *procedure name* or *label*

30. Try another run and make sure the application still works. If it does, try switching back and forth between the two options.

31. Save as `selsrt`.

32. Exit Visual Basic.

Alphabetization

Visual Basic uses the *ASCII* (pronounced *askee*, for American Standards Code for Information Interchange) character set, which is a 7-bit binary digit code ranging from binary 0000000 to 1111111 ("bit" comes from *binary digit*.) The decimal equivalents of these binary numbers are 0 and 127. It follows that the ASCII character set consists of 128 characters. For example, the binary code for the letter A is 1000001 or 65 in decimal notation. This code is designed to follow the ordering of the alphabet. The binary code for the letter B in decimal is 66, hence the letter A is "less than" the letter B. Consequently, it makes sense to write statements such as N$<M$; that is,

string variables can be compared in the same way as numbers. The word APPLE would be less than the word BUTTER since A is less than B. If two words begin with the same letter, then the computer automatically proceeds to the second letter of each word. Hence, ANIMAL is less than APPLE since N is less than P. If the first two letters are the same, it compares the third letters of each word and so on. For comparisons between names like SMITH, A. and SMITH, EDW., the computer would treat the first as less than the second because the commas would be equal and A comes before E in the ASCII character set. This ordering among string variables makes it possible to alphabetize a list of names.

To illustrate, let's alphabetize the list of employees in our payroll program. The first thing we must do is attach subscripts to the variables EmplName$, Hours, and HrRate, which we did earlier in this unit.

```
Sub cmdPayRol_Click ()
' Initialize employee counter and the total payroll accumulator
Empl = 0
Total = 0
Picture1.Print "Employee"; Tab(15); "Hours"; Tab(26); "Rate"; Tab(35); ⤷
        "Gross Pay"
Do Until EOF(1)
        Empl = Empl + 1
        Input #1, EmplName(Empl), Hours(Empl), HrRate(Empl)
        Wages(Empl) = Hours(Empl) * HrRate(Empl)
        Total = Total + Wages(Empl)
        Picture1.Print Tab(2); EmplName(Empl); Tab(15); Hours(Empl); ⤷
            Tab(25); HrRate(Empl); Tab(35); Format$(Wages(Empl), "currency")
Loop
Picture1.Print "The Total Payroll for the Week is "; Format$(Total, ⤷
        "currency")
End Sub
```

Second, to alphabetize the list of employees, we'll add an alphabetizing general procedure that will use the selection sort to alphabetize the names. This procedure will follow the cmdSelSrt procedure of the previous example. However, in this case we must remember to switch Hours, HrRate, and Wages each time we switch a name. *Otherwise, we will mix up the values while alphabetizing the names.*

To make the code more readable, we take this opportunity to introduce *subroutines*. A subroutine is a segment of code within a procedure designed to accomplish a specific task. It can only be used within the procedure in which it is defined. It is particularly useful when the same task needs to be performed several times from different locations in a procedure. A subroutine is identified by a *label*. This label is used by the GoSub statement to activate the subroutine. After its execution, the Return statement causes the run to continue from the line immediately following the corresponding GoSub. The rules for labeling a subroutine are as follows:

- The label must be on a line by itself.

- A label contains from 1 to 40 letters and/or digits, with no blank spaces, and must begin with a letter.

- A label must terminate with a colon (:).

For our current project, we use a subroutine to do all of the swapping when we alphabetize the list of employees. We call our subroutine SwapItems and show it below as part of the alphabetizing procedure.

Next, we adapt the selection sort routine to alphabetize the employees' names. Following the cmdSelSrt procedure of the sorting application, we create a general procedure to sort the names.

Code for the General Procedure to Alphabetize Employee List

```
Sub Selsort ()
For I = 1 To Empl - 1
    X = EmplName(I)
    K = I
    For J = I + 1 To Empl
        If EmplName(J) < X Then
        X = EmplName(J)
        hr = Hours(J)
        hrate = HrRate(J)
        w = Wages(J)
        k = J
        End If
    Next J
    Rem Swap names, hours, etc.
    GoSub SwapItems
Next I
Exit Sub
SwapItems:
Rem This subroutine swaps names, hours, etc.
    EmplName(k) = EmplName(I)
    EmplName(I) = X
    Hours(k) = Hours(I)
    Hours(I) = hr
    HrRate(k) = HrRate(I)
    HrRate(I) = hrate
    Wages(k) = Wages(I)
    Wages(I) = w
Return
End Sub
```

To call the general procedure Selsort, we simply place its name at the point where we want it be executed as shown in boldface in the modified cmdPayRol procedure listed here. You can also use the Call keyword to call Selsort.

Code for cmdPayRol with Alphabetizing

```
Sub cmdPayRol_Click ()
    Empl = 0
    Total = 0
Do Until EOF(1)
    Empl = Empl + 1
    Input #1, EmplName(Empl), Hours(Empl), HrRate(Empl)
    Wages(Empl) = Hours(Empl) * HrRate(Empl)
    Total = Total + Wages(Empl)
Loop
    Selsort
    Picture1.Print "Employee"; Tab(15); "Hours"; Tab(26); "Rate"; ↵
        Tab(35); "Gross Pay"
    Picture1.Print
For i = 1 To Empl
    Picture1.Print Tab(2); EmplName(i); Tab(15); Hours(i); Tab(25); ↵
        HrRate(i); Tab(35); Format$(Wages(i), "currency")
Next i
    Picture1.Print "The Total Payroll for the Week is "; ↵
        Format$(Total, "currency")
End Sub
```

Finally, to complete the application, we list the code for the Declarations section and for the Form_Load procedure.

Code for the Declarations Section

```
Dim EmplName(6) As String, Empl
Dim Hours(6), HrRate(6), Wages(6), Total
```

NOTE *These variables must be declared at the module level so that they will be visible to all procedures within the module.*

Code for Form_Load

```
Sub Form_Load ()
    Open "payrol.dat" For Input As #1
End Sub
```

GUIDED ACTIVITY 6.3

Alphabetizing

New features of Visual Basic contained in this activity:

- GoSub statement
- Return statement

- Subroutines

This activity demonstrates subroutines as well as the alphabetizing of a list of names.

1. Start Visual Basic.

2. Open the payrol.mak project you saved in Guided Activity 4.1.

3. Modify cmdPayRol to match the code given above.

4. Switch to (general) and enter the code for the Declarations section.

5. Select New Procedure from the View drop-down menu.

6. Enter `Selsort` in the Name box.

7. Click OK.

8. Enter the code for Selsort.

CHECKPOINT 6B What is the purpose of the Exit Sub statement immediately before the subroutine label?

9. Run the application to make sure it works. The output should be in alphabetical order.

10. Save as `payroll`.

11. Exit Visual Basic.

Using the Printer for Output

If you have a printer connected to your system, then Visual Basic treats it as an *object* called *Printer*. As an object it is accessed with the keyword Printer, and the Print method is used to direct output to it. For instance, no matter what value (numerical or string) *variablename* has, the statement

```
Printer.Print "The value is ", variablename
```

will send the message in quotes and this value to the printer. Since we are applying the Print method to the printer object, all of the rules concerning print zones, commas, semicolons, Tab, and Spc discussed earlier are still valid.

The Print Manager in Windows releases only full pages to the printer. When the *EndDoc method* is executed, the computer releases any pending printer output immediately to the printer and, therefore, it should be executed when all printing is complete. Without an EndDoc statement, the printer will not print, that is, it will not form feed the document until the run is terminated.

The EndDoc Method—Syntax

```
Printer.EndDoc
```

To illustrate, let's write a procedure to print the output of our payroll application. We'll call this new procedure cmdPrinter_Click () and attach it to a command button captioned "Print." To make sure the user does not try to click the Print button *before* clicking the Payroll button, we make it *invisible* until all of the calculations are complete by setting the **Visible property** to "False" at design time. The button can be made to reappear by setting the Visible property to "True" at the end of the cmdPayRol_Click procedure with the following statement.

```
cmdPrinter.Visible = True
```

To create cmdPrinter_Click (), we first copy all of the Picture1.Print statements into the print procedure and then change `Picture1` to `Printer` in each statement. This can be done easily using the Replace option in the Edit menu. We'll show how to do this in the next Guided Activity. Next, we add a Printer.EndDoc statement at the end of the other print statements. Finally, we use the **MsgBox function** (we use the function because we want a response from the user) to prompt the user to make sure the printer is turned on. The complete procedure is shown next.

Code for the cmdPrinter Procedure

```
Sub cmdPrinter_Click ()
    Ans = MsgBox("Is the printer turned on?", 33, "Print Option")
    If Ans = 2 Then
        Exit Sub
    End If
    Printer.Print "Employee"; Tab(15); "Hours"; Tab(26); "Rate"; ↵
        Tab(35); "Gross Pay"
    Printer.Print
    For i = 1 To Empl
        Printer.Print Tab(2); EmplName(i); Tab(15); Hours(i); Tab(25); ↵
            HrRate(i); Tab(35); Format$(Wages(i), "currency")
    Next i
    Printer.Print "The Total Payroll for the Week is "; Format$(Total, ↵
        "currency")
    Printer.EndDoc
End Sub
```

GUIDED ACTIVITY 6.4

Using the Printer

New features of Visual Basic contained in this activity:

- MsgBox function
- Printer object
- Visible property

This activity is designed to show how to get a printer (if one is available) to print the output of an application.

1. Start Visual Basic.

2. Open the payrol1.mak project.

3. Draw a command button next to the Payroll button.

4. Change the caption on this button to `Print`, its name to `cmdPrinter`, and set the Visible property to False.

5. Open the Code window for cmdPayRol_Click ( ) .

6. Enter the following line immediately before the End Sub statement.

   ```
   cmdPrinter.Visible = True
   ```

7. Open the Code window for cmdPrinter_Click ( ) .

8. Enter the following code segment.

   ```
   Ans = MsgBox("Is the printer turned on?", 33, "Print Option")
   If Ans = 2 Then
        Exit Sub
   End If
   ```

9. Switch to cmdPayRol.

10. Highlight and copy the two Picture1.Print statements below the call to SelSort.

11. Switch to cmdPrinter and paste these two lines below the ones entered in step 8.

12. Switch back to cmdPayRol and copy the entire For/Next loop.

13. Paste these lines into cmdPrinter.

14. Switch back to cmdPayRol and copy the Picture1.Print line immediately above EndSub.

15. Paste this line into cmdPrinter, immediately *following* Next i.

16. Click the Edit title on the menu bar and select Replace.

17. Enter `Picture1` in the Find What box and press ⌗Tab⌗.

18. Enter `Printer` in the Replace With box and click the Replace All button (be sure Current Procedure is the selected option).

19. Enter a Printer.EndDoc statement immediately before the End Sub.

20. This completes the program additions, so now you can try a run.

21. Click the Print button to make sure the cmdPrinter procedure works correctly.

22. Save as `payrol2`.

23. Exit Visual Basic.

About the New Features in Guided Activity 6.4

Now that you have seen the program run, you should understand how the Visible property works. This is a good way to keep a user from clicking the wrong button. The MsgBox function is distinguished from the MsgBox statement by the use of parentheses. The function returns a value to the program that explains why it is used in an assignment statement. The type number 33 was obtained by adding together the type number (1) for the OK and Cancel options to the type number (32) for a question mark. We did this to make it possible for the user to change their mind about printing after clicking the Print button. Consult the *Language Reference* for more information on type numbers.

Two-Dimensional Arrays

The number of subscripts in a variable name is not limited to one. Double-subscripted variables are permitted and are used to denote a *two-dimensional array* called a *matrix*. A matrix is simply a collection of numbers arranged into a rectangle consisting of one or more rows and one or more columns. Here is an example of a 3-by-2 matrix:

$$\begin{pmatrix} 3 & 7 \\ 4 & 0 \\ 2 & 3 \end{pmatrix}$$

We call this a 3-by-2 matrix because it has three rows (horizontal) and two columns (vertical). The following is a 2-by-4 matrix:

$$\begin{pmatrix} -1 & 2 & 7 & 9 \\ 0 & 9 & 2 & 5 \end{pmatrix}$$

Matrices occur quite naturally in many contexts. Consider, for example, Table 6.2.

TABLE 6.2
Catch of fish (tons)

COUNTRY	FRESH-WATER FISH	SALMON	FLOUNDER	COD	REDFISH	HERRING	TUNA	OTHER
Peru	10	0	1	421	51	2234	12	58
U.S.	46	187	90	122	117	1278	194	295
Canada	21	85	161	393	87	324	5	91
Chile	0	0	0	23	17	808	5	257
Brazil	131	0	2	29	220	217	3	164
Mexico	15	0	1	4	63	182	32	314
Argentina	10	0	2	351	55	17	2	34

The numbers in this table form the following 7-by-8 matrix.

$$\begin{pmatrix}
10 & 0 & 1 & 421 & 51 & 2234 & 12 & 58 \\
46 & 187 & 90 & 122 & 117 & 1278 & 194 & 295 \\
21 & 85 & 161 & 393 & 87 & 324 & 5 & 91 \\
0 & 0 & 0 & 23 & 17 & 808 & 5 & 257 \\
131 & 0 & 2 & 29 & 220 & 217 & 3 & 164 \\
15 & 0 & 1 & 4 & 63 & 182 & 32 & 314 \\
10 & 0 & 2 & 351 & 55 & 17 & 2 & 34
\end{pmatrix}$$

Each row represents the catch of fish for a country, and each column the catch of a particular kind of fish. We will now explain how to:

- Read the matrix into the computer
- Display the matrix
- Find the sum of each column
- Find the sum of each row
- Display any individual entry in the matrix
- Find the maximum value in any given column

We begin by reading the matrix into the computer as a two-dimensional array called fish.

A Procedure to Read the Catch of Fish Matrix

```
For row = 1 To 7
    For col = 1 to 9
        Input #1 fish(row,col)
    Next col
Next row
```

The country names and the matrix, written above, become the file data for this procedure.

```
Peru, 10, 0, 1, 421, 51, 2234, 12, 58
U.S., 46, 187, 90, 122, 117, 1278, 194, 295
Canada, 21, 85, 161, 393, 87, 324, 5, 91
Chile, 0, 0, 0, 23, 17, 808, 5, 257
Brazil, 131, 0, 2, 29, 220, 217, 3, 164
Mexico, 15, 0, 1, 4, 63, 182, 32, 314
Argentina, 10, 0, 2, 351, 55, 17, 2, 34
```

We use the following Dim statement to create the double-subscripted array called fish.

```
Dim fish(1 To 7, 1 To 9)
```

The first subscript range always refers to the rows and the second to the columns. Thus, this array consists of 7 X 9 = 63 memory cells, one for the country and one for each entry in the matrix.

It should be clear that, when we refer to this array in program statements, the first subscript points to a row and the second points to a column. Hence, with row=3 and col=5, fish(3,5) would be 393—the entry in the third row and the fifth column. That is, fish(3,5) is the catch of cod in Canada. The procedure reads the matrix by rows. The Next row statement controls the row number, and the Next col statement the column number. The control variable row starts with a value of 1 and remains 1 until col runs from 1 to 9; then row becomes a 2 and col starts over at 1, running again to 9, and so on until row exceeds 7. Thus, for each value of row, the computer reads the 9 values fish(1,1), fish(1,2), fish(1,3), ..., fish(1,9) as Peru, 10, 0, 1, 421, 51, 2234, 12, 58, respectively; it then reads fish(2,1), fish(2,2), fish(2,3), ..., fish(2,8) as U.S., 46, 187, 90, 122, 117, 1278, 194, 295, respectively, and so on until the entire matrix has been read.

To display the matrix, we use the procedure cmdDisplayTable_Click ( ) shown next.

A Procedure to Display a Matrix

```
Sub cmdDisplayTable_Click ()
For row = 1 To 7
    Picture1.Print Format$(fish(row, 1), "@@@@@@@@@!"); Spc(1);
    For col = 2 To 9
        Picture1.Print Format$(fish(row, col), "@@@@@");
    Next col
    Picture1.Print
Next row
End Sub
```

To make the output from the cmdDisplayTable procedure come out neatly in nice straight rows and columns, we used the formatting character @. As we have seen before, this character placeholder prints the character in the given position if there is a character, otherwise it fills the position with a space. The character ! (see first Format$) forces the placeholders to be filled in from *left to right* rather than from *right to left*. We used this character (!) in the format string for the countries so that they would be left-justified. For more information on formatting characters, consult the *Language Reference*.

Our next task is to find the sum of the columns and the rows. We assume that the matrix has been entered as fish(i,j).

To sum the columns, we use the following procedure.

A Procedure to Sum the Columns

```
Sub Colsum ()
    For i = 2 To 9
        Csum = 0
        For j = 1 To 7
            Csum = Csum + fish(j, i)
```

```
            Next j
            Clsum(i) = Csum
        Next i
End Sub
```

After executing this procedure the computer will have the sum of each column stored in the one-dimensional array Clsum(i).

A Procedure to Sum the Rows

```
Sub Rowsum ()
    For i = 1 To 7
        Rsum = 0
        For j = 2 To 9
            Rsum = Rsum + fish(i, j)
        Next j
        Rwsum(i) = Rsum
    Next i
End Sub
```

After this module is executed, the sum of each row will be stored in the one-dimensional array Rwsum(i).

An Application to Extract Information from Table 6.2

In this application, we permit the user to extract any piece of information contained in the table by choosing a country and a type of fish. Each of these selections will be made by means of a *list box*. A list box contains a list of choices that may be selected with the mouse or by the arrow keys. If the list of items is longer than what can be displayed, a scroll bar is automatically added to the box. To draw a list box on a form, select the List Box icon in the Toolbox (the fifth item in the right column). The *AddItem method* is used to add an item to a list box.

AddItem Method—Syntax

*object.*AddItem *item*

We use two list boxes in this application, one for the country and one for the kind of fish. Their default names are List1 and List2, respectively. To place the items in the boxes, we use the following code in the Form_Load procedure. For the list of countries, we use

```
List1.AddItem "Peru"
List1.AddItem "U.S."
List1.AddItem "Canada"
List1.AddItem "Chile"
List1.AddItem "Brazil"
List1.AddItem "Mexico"
List1.AddItem "Argentina"
```

and for the kinds of fish, we use

```
List2.AddItem "Fresh-water fish"
List2.AddItem "Salmon"
List2.AddItem "Flounder"
List2.AddItem "Cod"
List2.AddItem "Redfish"
List2.AddItem "Herring"
List2.AddItem "Tuna"
List2.AddItem "Other"
```

The values of the current selections are stored in the variable List1.Text and List2.Text. When the user clicks on a box choice, the code in the corresponding click event procedure is executed. In the case of a country, we want to set the row index to the row number of the selected country, and for a kind of fish, we want to set the column index to the corresponding column. Here is the code.

Code for List1_Click ()

```
Sub List1_Click ()
    Select Case list1.Text
        Case "Peru"
        row = 1
        Case "U.S."
        row = 2
        Case "Canada"
        row = 3
        Case "Chile"
        row = 4
        Case "Brazil"
        row = 5
        Case "Mexico"
        row = 6
        Case "Argentina"
        row = 7
    End Select
End Sub
```

Code for List2_Click ()

```
Sub List2_Click ()
    Select Case list2.Text
        Case "Fresh-water fish"
        col = 2
        Case "Salmon"
        col = 3
        Case "Flounder"
        col = 4
```

```
        Case "Cod"
          col = 5
        Case "Redfish"
          col = 6
        Case "Herring"
          col = 7
        Case "Tuna"
          col = 8
        Case "Other"
          col = 9
      End Select
  End Sub
```

Next, we create a procedure that takes the values of row and col that have been set by the two procedures List1_Click and List2_Click and prints the corresponding matrix entry.

Code for the Catch Button

```
  Sub cmdCatch_Click ()
      If list1.Text = "" Or list2.Text = "" Then
          MsgBox "You must select a country and a kind of fish"
          Exit Sub
      End If
      Picture1.Cls
      Picture1.Print "The number of tons of "; list2.Text
      Picture1.Print "caught in "; list1.Text; " was "; fish(row, col)
  End Sub
```

GUIDED ACTIVITY 6.5

Extracting Information from Table 6.2

New features of Visual Basic contained in this activity:

- @ format character

- List boxes

- Two-dimensional arrays

    This activity elicits certain kinds of information from the data given in Table 6.2.

1. Open Notepad.

2. Enter the given data including the names of the countries, as shown in Table 6.2.

3. Save the file as fish.dat.

4. Start Visual Basic.

5. Enter the following dimension statements in the Declarations section.

```
Dim fish(1 To 7, 1 To 9)
Dim Rwsum(7), Clsum(2 To 9)
Dim row As Integer, col As Integer
```

CHECKPOINT 6C Why do the subscripts for Clsum run from 2 to 9?

6. Choose New Procedure from the drop-down menu for the View title on the menu bar.

7. Enter `Colsum` in the Name box and click OK.

8. Enter the given code for Colsum.

9. Repeat steps 6, 7, and 8 for the Rowsum procedure.

10. Draw the user interface as shown in Figure 6.5.

FIGURE 6.5
User interface for Guided Activity 6.5

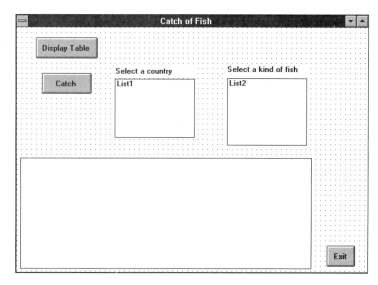

11. Change the name of the Display Table button to `cmdDisplayTable`.

12. Enter the given code for cmdDisplayTable_Click ().

13. Name the Catch button `cmdCatch` and enter the given code.

14. Open the Code window for the form.

15. Enter the following code.

```
Open "fish.dat" For Input As #1
For row = 1 To 7
     For col = 1 To 9
          Input #1, fish(row, col)
     Next col
Next row
```

FIGURE 6.6

*Beginning of a
run of Guided
Activity 6.5*

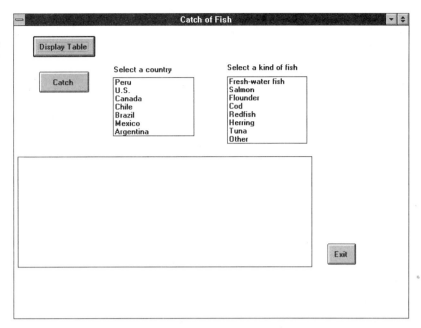

16. Enter the given code to create the contents of the two list boxes.

17. Open the Code window for the Exit button and enter

```
Close #1
End
```

18. Start a run by pressing [F5]. See Figure 6.6.

19. Click the Display Table button.

20. Select Canada in the first list box.

21. Select Tuna in the second list box.

22. Click the Catch button. The output should be 5 tons.

23. Try several other combinations of countries and fish.

24. Add another command button, below the Catch button, captioned `Total Catch by Country`, and name it `cmdTotCatch`.

25. Enter the following code into this procedure.

```
Sub cmdTotCatch_Click ()
    If list1.Text = "" Then
        MsgBox "You must select a country"
        Exit Sub
    End If
    Call Rowsum
    Picture1.Cls
    Picture1.Print "The number of tons caught in "; list1.Text
    Picture1.Print "was "; Rwsum(row)
End Sub
```

26. Start a run and use this new button to check the total tonnage by country. The total for Peru is 2787.

27. Add another command button just below the Total Catch by Country button captioned `Total Catch by Kind of Fish` and name it `cmdTotFish`.

28. Enter the following code into this procedure.

```
Sub cmdTotFish_Click ()
    If list2.Text = "" Then
        MsgBox "You must select a kind of fish"
        Exit Sub
    End If
    Call Colsum
    Picture1.Cls
    Picture1.Print "The number of tons of "; list2.Text
    Picture1.Print "caught was "; Clsum(col)
End Sub
```

29. Start a run and check the total tonnage for tuna. It should be 253 tons.

30. Check some other totals of your own choosing.

31. Save the application as `ga6-5`.

32. Exit Visual Basic.

About the New Features in Guided Activity 6.5.

The *List property* for a list box is an array containing each item in the list in string form. Each item is assigned an index with 0 being the smallest index and n-1 the largest where n is the number of items in the box. Through this property, every item in the box can be accessed by its index.

The List Property—Syntax

object.List*(index)*

For example, the statement

```
Picture1.Print List1.List(2)
```

would print Canada as the *third* item in the first list box, and

```
Picture1.Print List2.List(4)
```

would print Redfish.

To remove an item from a list box, use the *RemoveItem method*.

RemoveItem Method—Syntax

object.RemoveItem *index*

In the RemoveItem method, *index* refers to the index assigned by the List property.

If you want the items in a list box to be sorted alphabetically, you can set the **Sorted property** to True in the Properties window. Be careful when using this property since the List property may produce an unexpected index. In the case of Guided Activity 6.5, the Sorted property can be set to True since the Select Case statements work by name, not by index. To see this property in action, start Visual Basic, load ga6-5, change the Sorted property to True on both list boxes, and run the program.

With a list box the user can only choose the listed items, and, since all of the items are displayed, a long list may take up too much space on the interface. A **combo box** eliminates both problems. It permits you to enter your own choice or select one from the displayed list. A combo box has three styles. The *drop-down combo box* (Style 0) contains an edit box and a drop-down list. You can type your choice in the edit box or click the arrow at the right end of the box and pick something from the drop-down list. The *simple combo box* (Style 1) contains only an edit box, and you must type your own choice The *drop-down list combo box* (Style 2) will only allow you to choose from a drop-down list. Items are added to a combo box in the same way as a list box, preferably in the Form_Load procedure. You will be asked to use a combo box in the Exercises.

How to Find the Maximum of a Column

Let's assume that the subscript for the column for which we want the maximum is denoted by col. We'll define Large as the variable used to store the largest value of that column and Rowmax as the corresponding row index. Since the first entry in the column may be the largest, we begin by setting Large equal to the first entry in row 1 and the given column and Rowmax = 1.

Next, we compare Large with each of the remaining entries in the column. If a larger entry is found, then Large is set to that value and the row subscript of the larger value is stored in Rowmax.

A Procedure for Finding the Largest Entry in a Given Column of Table 6.2

```
Rem Large will hold the largest value and initially it is the first
Rem entry in the column
Large = fish(1,col)
Rowmax = 1
Rem Compare Large with the remaining entries in the column
For j = 2 To 7
    If Large < fish(j, col) Then
        Large = fish(j,col)
        Rowmax = j    ' Remember the row index of new value for Large
    End If
Next j
```

GUIDED ACTIVITY 6.6

Extracting Additional Information from Table 6.2

New features of Visual Basic contained in this activity:

- Combo boxes
- List property

In this activity we try out the procedure for finding the country with the largest catch of a particular kind of fish.

1. Start Visual Basic.

2. Open the project you saved at the end of Guided Activity 6.5 called ga6-5.mak.

3. To illustrate the List property, open the Code window for cmdTotCatch.

4. Replace list1.Text with list1.List(row-1) (recall that the list index runs from 0 to 6).

5. Start a run. The program should run in exactly the same way as before the change.

6. Stop the run and draw a command button on the form captioned Maximum Catch by Fish.

7. Name the new button cmdMaxFish.

8. Open the Code window for cmdMaxFish_Click ( ).

9. Enter the following code.

```
Sub cmdMaxFish_Click ()
    If List1.Text = "" Then
        MsgBox "You must select a kind of fish"
        Exit Sub
    End If
    Large = fish(1, col)
    Rowmax = 1
    For j = 2 To 7
        If Large < fish(j, col) Then
            Large = fish(j, col)
            Rowmax = j
        End If
    Next j
    Picture1.Cls
    Picture1.Print "The largest catch of "; List1.Text; " was"
    Picture1.Print Large; "tons caught by "; fish(Rowmax, 1)
End Sub
```

10. Start a run and verify that the new command button gives the correct results.

11. Stop the run by clicking the Exit button.

12. Next, we illustrate the use of a combo box. Activate the List2.box by clicking it on the form.

13. Press ⟦Del⟧.

14. Click the Combo box icon in the Toolbox. It is the fifth icon in the left-hand column of the Toolbox.

15. Draw a combo box in the same place as the List2 box you just deleted.

16. Open the Code window for Form_Load.

17. Change List2 to Combo1 in the entire project using the Replace command in the Edit menu.

18. Start a run and observe the operation of the combo box. The style setting for this box is 0, the default value.

19. Stop the run by clicking the Exit button.

20. Open the Properties window for the combo box.

21. Change the combo box style to 2—Dropdown List.

22. Run again and observe how this new style works.

23. Save the form as ga6-6.frm and the project as ga6-6.mak.

24. Exit Visual Basic.

Keyword Syntax Review

Keyword—Syntax	Purpose
object.AddItem *item*	To add an item to a list box or a combo box
[Call] *procedure name* or *label*	To execute the procedure named

Dim *array name* (*largest subscript*)
    As *type*
        or
Dim *array name* (*smallest subscript*
    To *largest subscript*) As *type*
	To allocate memory locations for arrays

GoSub *label*	To execute the subroutine identified by the label
Printer	To access the Printer object
Printer.EndDoc	To terminate data sent to the printer, releasing it to the printer
ReDim *array name*(*subscripts*)	To allocate or reallocate storage space for an array
object.RemoveItem *index*	To remove an item from a list box or a combo box
Return	To return control of a program to the statement following the corresponding GoSub

EXERCISE 6.1

Table Analysis

The purpose of this exercise is to continue the analysis of Table 6.2, Catch of Fish, started in Guided Activity 6.5.

1. Modify cmdTotFish_Click to also print the average tonnage of a particular fish caught.

2. Modify cmdTotCatch_Click to also print the average tonnage by country.

3. Write a procedure and integrate it into project ga6-5 that will determine the maximum tonnage for each country. Have the procedure print the name of each country, the maximum tonnage, and the corresponding kind of fish.

4. Write a procedure and integrate it into project ga6-5 that will determine the minimum tonnage for each country. Have the procedure print the name of each country, the minimum tonnage, and the corresponding kind of fish.

5. Write a procedure and integrate it into project ga6-5 that will determine the maximum tonnage for each kind of fish. Have the procedure print the name of each fish, the maximum tonnage, and the corresponding country.

6. Write a procedure and integrate it into project ga6-5 that will determine the minimum tonnage by kind of fish. Have the procedure print the name of each fish, the minimum tonnage, and the corresponding country.

EXERCISE 6.2

Average Charge Sale

B&J TV wants to estimate the average amount of a charge sale and the percentage of charges above the average. To do this, they select a random sample of 14 charge sales from the current week. The average is computed and a count of the number of sales greater than the average is determined. Next, the percentage of sales greater than the average is computed.

After designing an interface, write a program to carry out the tasks outlined above. Test your program with the following data.

Test Data:

34.9, 99.13, 13, 13, 63.71, 12, 17.6, 50.81, 18.87, 42.84, 25.16, 97.27, 25, 15.49

The total is $528.79, the average is $37.77, and the percentage of the sample over the average is 35.71%.

EXERCISE 6.3

Mutual Fund Portfolio (I)

An investor has a mutual fund portfolio containing 12 funds. The number of shares in each fund is stored in a file called shares.dat and the market price of each fund is stored in another file called value.dat. To compute the present market value of a fund, multiply the number of shares in the fund by the corresponding market price. The total market value of the portfolio is the sum of these present market values. After designing an interface, write a program to compute the present value of each fund, and the total market value of the portfolio. Use two one-dimensional arrays to hold the number of shares and the market prices. Using command buttons, give the user the options of either displaying on the screen or printing a table containing the number of shares, the corresponding market prices, the present value of each fund, and the total market value of the portfolio.

Test your program using the following data.

shares.dat

1654, 938.36, 658.42, 163, 12740, 328, 1841.965, 2020, 391, 771, 1601, 199

value.dat

2.66, 11.61, 25.55, 22.49, 6.62, 14.34, 18.13, 14.58, 17.55, 6.56, 6.63, 18.31

EXERCISE 6.4

Mutual Fund Portfolio (II)

Revise your solution to Exercise 6.3 to allow the user to update the number of shares and the market values before printing or displaying the table described there. These updates can be carried out by means of the array index. If there are any updates, then have the program rewrite the files before exiting the program. To rewrite a file, you must close it first and then reopen it for output. Make up several updates to test your program.

EXERCISE 6.5

Total Sales Report (I)

Barron's Market uses a computer to keep track of the daily sales for its 12 branch stores. At closing time, each branch enters the total daily receipts into the computer and a sales file is created. The computer reads this file and prints out a sales report. Write a program to read the sales file and print the report. The report should include the total sales for all branches.

Test Data:

556.58, 7480, 6969, 1947, 2611, 3541.23, 991.45, 10440.42. 5480.61, 6480.91, 17540.51, 9841.68

EXERCISE 6.6

Total Sales Report (II)

Revise your solution to Exercise 6.5 so that the user may choose to have the sales report printed with the sales in descending order along with the corresponding branch number. The following is a partial report.

Branch	Sales
9	$17,540.51
8	$10,440.42
12	$ 9,841.68
etc.	

EXERCISE 6.7

Foreign Exchange

Suppose the following international exchange rates are in effect at the present time:

INTERNATIONAL EXCHANGE RATES

****

Country	Currency Unit	Dollars per Currency Unit

****

Country	Currency Unit	Dollars per Currency Unit
Australia	Dollar	0.7675
Bolivia	Peso	0.052
Canada	Dollar	0.86
China	Renminbi	0.61
France	Franc	0.235
Germany	Mark	0.52
Italy	Lira	0.01214
Japan	Yen	0.01006
Russia	Ruble	1.5
United Kingdom	Pound	1.98

For example, 1 Japanese yen is worth .01006 cents (about a cent).

Design an interface and write an application using a combo box (Style 2) containing the countries shown. Provide a command button to allow the user to display a conversion table after selecting a country from the combo box. If the dollars per currency unit are less than $0.50, then the conversion table should run from 100 to 900 in steps of 100, and from 1000 to 9000 in steps of 1000. Otherwise, the list of the currency should vary from 1 to 9, and from 10 to 90 in steps of 10. For example, the table should appear as shown here for Japan.

Yen	U.S. Dollars	Yen	U.S. Dollars
100	$1.01	1000	$10.06
200	$2.01	2000	$20.12
300	$3.02	3000	$30.18
400	$4.02	4000	$40.24
etc.			

Be sure to give the user the option of sending the table to the printer.

EXERCISE 6.8

Inventory

The following inventory table is to be used as test data for this exercise.

Model #	Serial #	Make	Cost	# in Stock
ICF-72	52117	SON	128.85	5
ICF-C11	54811	SON	59.54	6
ACT-T16	56711	PAN	149.95	15
TKE-112	89C12	PAN	89.50	10
RC-6015	10472	REG	189.95	25
KV-1923	8855	SON	249.95	2
KPF-102	5666	TVC	549.95	13
BT-115	12551	ARV	25.85	15
TBA-112	55671	PAN	125.00	12
DEF-112	D1123	JVC	89.45	17

1. Write a procedure that will read from a file the data contained in the above table into five arrays.

2. Write a procedure that will reproduce the above table.

3. Write a procedure that will print the table in alphabetical order by model number.

4. Write a procedure that will print the table in alphabetical order by make.

5. Write a procedure that permits the user to obtain the table information for a given make.

6. Write a module that accepts, through an InputBox$ statement, a model number and then displays the table information for that particular model. Be sure your module is able to handle the case where a user has entered a model number that is not in the table.

7. Design an interface and combine your solution to parts 1 to 6 into one program and test it.

EXERCISE 6.9

Multiple Choice Examination Grading

Our goal in this exercise is to create a program that could be used to grade a multiple choice examination containing N questions.

1. Write a procedure to read from a file the number of questions, the number of students, an array of correct answers, an array of student names, and their answers to the questions into a two-dimensional array.

    Sample Data:

    Number of Questions: 20
    Number of Students: 4
    Correct Answers: 5, 1, 4, 3, 5, 3, 5, 1, 1, 3, 3, 4, 4, 5, 5, 1, 2, 4, 1, 5
    KNIGHT, 5, 1, 4, 3, 5, 3, 5, 1, 1, 3, 3, 4, 4, 5, 5, 1, 2, 4, 1, 5
    GILL, 5, 2, 5, 3, 5, 2, 4, 1, 1, 2, 3, 4, 3, 3, 5, 1, 2, 4, 1, 5
    JONES, 1, 3, 5, 3, 5, 2, 4, 1, 1, 2, 3, 4, 3, 3, 5, 1, 2, 4, 1, 5
    SMITH, 5, 1, 4, 3, 1, 2, 4, 1, 1, 1, 3, 5, 3, 3, 1, 1, 2, 4, 1, 5

2. Write a procedure to be used with your solution to part 1 that will determine the number of correct answers and output the percentage right and the percentage wrong for each student.

3. Write a procedure that will print the names in alphabetical order and the final grades. The final grade is the percentage right.

4. Write a procedure that will compute, for each question, the number who got it right and the corresponding percentage of students.

5. Design an interface and combine all of the procedures into a single program, and then test it.

EXERCISE 6.10

TV Poll

Consider the following results of a poll of 12 viewers.

Viewer	Sex (1=female, 2=male)	Top 10 Shows in Order of Preference
1	1	A, J, D, B, C, G, I, F, E, H
2	1	H, A, D, C, B, G, I, E, F, J
3	2	A, J, D, I, F, E, H, D, B, C
4	2	C, D, A, I, E, F, H, B, J, G
5	1	B, C, A, I, F, E, G, H, J, D
6	2	A, J, D, F, E, I, G, H, B, C
7	1	C, D, J, I, F, G, H, E, A, B
8	2	A, B, J, D, C, F, H, G, E, I
9	2	B, C, A, I, J, D, F, E, G, H
10	1	J, G, H, B, A, C, D, F, E, I

| 11 | 1 | A, D, E, F, B, C, H, I, G, J |
| 12 | 1 | A, J, H, B, I, D, C, E, F, G |

Each viewer was given a list of 10 TV shows coded by A through J and asked to put them in order of preference, starting with his or her favorite show and ending with the least favorite. For example, viewer 1 is a female whose favorite show is show A, her second choice is J, and so on. Viewer 9 is a male whose favorite show is B and whose least favorite is H.

1. Write a procedure that will read from a file the sex of the viewer into a one-dimensional array and the show preferences into a two-dimensional array.

2. Write a procedure that will rank the 10 shows as determined by the 12 viewers. The output should appear as follows.

Rank	Show	# of Votes	Percentage
1	A	6	50
2	J	4	40
etc.			

3. Write a procedure to find the top three shows among the female viewers.

4. Design an interface and combine all of the procedures into a single program, and then test it.

Review Questions

1. Explain the difference between a static array and a dynamic array.

*2. Explain why strings can be compared in the same manner as numbers.

*3. Why are Dim statements required for arrays?

4. How many storage locations are set aside by the following statement?

    ```
    Dim A(30)
    ```

5. How many variable names are established by Dim FName$(1 To 15)?

6. If N = 5, how many memory locations are designated by Dim Element(2 * N)?

*7. Are the variables A(2) and A2 the same? Why or why not?

8. Which of the following variable names are valid with respect to Dim A(1 To 15)?

    (i) A(1);   (ii) A(0);   (iii) A15;   (iv) A(31)

9. The selection sort method may be divided into steps where a step consists of one complete trip through the loop. At the end of each step, what has happened to the list of numbers?

10. By "playing computer," explain why the first four grades are zeros but the last grade is 1471 in the output from the following code. There is more than one error. What would you do to correct this program?

```
For K = 1 To 5
    S = 0
    For J = 1 To 4
        Input #1 G
        A = A + G
    Next J
    S(J) = A
Next K
For Z = 1 To 5
    Print "Average Grade for # ";Z:" = ";S(Z)
Next Z
```

Contents of data file #1:

86,90,40,50,60,70,70,75,80,85,90,70,75,85,77,82,98,72,56,60

The output is

```
Average Grade for #1 = 0
Average Grade for #2 = 0
Average Grade for #3 = 0
Average Grade for #4 = 0
Average Grade for #5 = 1471
```

*11.   Consider the following program.

```
For J = 1 To 5
    A = 0
    For I = 1 To 4
        Input #1 X
        A = A + X
    Next I
    A(I) = A / 4
Next J
Print "The output"
For K = 1 To 5
    Print A(K);
Next K
```

Contents of data file #1:

2,3,4,5,6,8,9,10,11,16,7,2,8,7,5,4,8,10,3,11

A run of this program produced the following output:

```
The output
0 0 0 0 8
```

Explain this output. What is the program supposed to do? What changes would you make to correct it?

12.   What is the purpose of the @ format character?

13. What is a list box?

14. What is the difference between a list box and a combo box?

Important Terms

AddItem method	Index	Pseudocode
Array	Label	RemoveItem method
ASCII	List box	Sorted property
Combo box	List property	Static array
Data structure	Matrix	Subroutine
Declarations section	MsgBox function	Subscript
Dynamic array	One-dimensional array	Two-dimensional array
EndDoc method	Pointer	Visible property
General procedure	Printer object	

Answers

Answers to Checkpoints

1A. Press [Alt][F4] or click anywhere on the form.

1B. Drag one of the sizing handles.

1C. By clicking on it.

1D. By dragging it with the mouse.

1E. By choosing the Caption property in the Properties window and typing the desired caption.

1F. Choose the Save File As command from the drop-down File menu and save the form and then choose the Save Project As command from the same menu and save the project. You may also simply click the Save File icon on the menu bar and supply the names you want for the two files.

2A. Click anywhere on the form, or click the Control-menu box of the window and select Close, or click View Form in the Project window.

2B. To exit from the program and stop the run.

3A. Double-click the button or use the View Code command in the Project window.

3B. Use the Object box and select the desired window.

3C. The icon on the toolbar that looks like a 3.5-inch floppy disk.

3D. Highlight the current value and type the new value.

3E. Select New Project in the File menu.

3F. An End statement.

4A. The icon that looks like a 3.5 inch floppy disk.

4B. To declare n as an integer and to make it visible to all procedures in the module.

4C. Press $\boxed{F7}$ and then select the desired object from the Object box, or double-click on the object.

4D. Choose Run from the Run menu or press $\boxed{F5}$.

5A. $\boxed{F4}$

5B. Yes, press $\boxed{Tab}$ until the Destination box has the focus, then use the arrow keys to select Philadelphia.

5C. Only when both component statements are true.

5D. It negates the statement. It changes True to False and False to True.

6A. Using the Object box in the Code window.

6B. This statement keeps the program from entering the subroutine without a GoSub statement.

6C. Because of the names, the numbers are in columns 2 through 9.

Answers to Review Questions

1-1.

T	A	B
15	15	30

T	A	B
15	30	30

T	A	B
15	30	15

They interchange the values of A and B.

1-3. Yes. It increases the value of N by one.

1-4.

A	B	C	D	S	T
4	36	9	109	25	100

1-5.

N	X	S
1	1	1

N	X	S
2	3	10

N	X	S
3	6	46

1-7. A window that displays the interface for the application.

1-10. It becomes the interface for your application without the dots.

1-13. It can be utilized to display a picture or text.

1-15. A label.

1-19. When set to True, the size of the label adjusts automatically to the size of the caption.

2-2.
```
Y = 2 + 25 * 2 / 5 ^ 2 / 5 / 4
  = 2 + 25 * 2 / 25 / 5 / 4
  = 2 + 50 / 25 / 5 / 4
  = 2 + 2 / 5 / 4
  = 2 + .4 / 4
  = 2 + .1 = 2.1
```

2-4. 14 characters.

2-6. Put a semicolon at the end of the line.

2-9. `"percent"`

2-10. $695.57

2-12. `txtTax.Text = Format$(Taxes, "currency")`

3-2. The first time the Do statement is executed, the condition N < 10 is true and consequently the loop is not executed. Change the condition to N > 10. The value of N is *never* changed, and therefore is never greater than 10. Correct the problem by adding the line `N = N + 1` within the loop.

3-3. When a sequence of statements needs to be executed several times.

3-5. A post-test loop is one where the condition that controls the loop is checked after the body of the loop has been executed.

3-12.
```
For I = 1 To 19 Step 2
    S = S + I
Next I
```

3-13. Once.

3-14. No.

4-3. Input, output, append.

4-5. To conclude the input or output to a file.

4-8. Input #

4-12. The number assigned to the file by the Open statement.

5-1. When Value is odd.

5-3. Switch the words EVEN and ODD.

5-4a. Change to X * Y > 0 for example.

5-4b. No comma permitted in an If/Then statement. Remove the comma.

5-4c. Condition –10 < X < 20 not written correctly. Change to –10 < X And X < 20.

5-4d. No error.

5-5. Larger.

5-7.
```
If X > 0 Then
      Print "X is Positive"
Else
    If X < 0 Then
          Print "X is Negative"
    Else
          Print "X = Zero"
    End If
End If
```

5-11. True.

5-13. 4.

5-16. Rounds X to the first integer greater than X if X >= 1.5. Otherwise, X remains the same.

5-18. To implement the multioption decision structure.

6-2. Because of the ASCII code, "A" is less than "B", etc.

6-3. Because QBasic only sets aside 11 memory cells for the array without the Dim statement. If an array contains more than 11 subscripts, a Dim statement is required.

6-7. A(2) is the second element of an array, whereas A2 is a single variable name not related to an array.

6-11. This program is supposed to compute the average value of every four numbers in the statement. To correct it, change I to J in the statement A(I) = A/4.

Index